Art in Bloom at Home

A Practical Guide to
Floral Design and Flower Care

By Carolyn H. Everitt

Illustrated by Jennie Lou Brockelman

Cover and Layout Design by Scotty Dolan

Museum of Fine Arts, Boston

Dedication

To Chuck Thomas, former Director of Membership for the Museum and the person known fondly by generations of Ladies Committee members as the father and creator of Art in Bloom.

And to Bruce, my husband and my best friend, who engineers my every idea with patience and understanding.

Table of Contents

Notes

Preface

Art in Bloom began in the spring of 1975 as a three-day festival of art and flowers to attract new visitors to the Museum of Fine Arts, Boston. That first year, former and current members of the Ladies Committee created sixteen arrangements to complement paintings that had been hung especially for the occasion in the lower rotunda and adjoining corridors.

A winning concept from the start, Art in Bloom has flourished over the years. Today, more than one hundred floral compositions are created by Boston area garden clubs and professional designers for what has become a very successful and widely imitated annual fund raiser.

In addition to presenting Art in Bloom each year, the Ladies Committee creates several thousand floral arrangements for display throughout the entire museum. The variety of requirements for these arrangements is enormous — bud vases for desks and cafe tables, small and large designs for the restaurant, eight-foot high designs at the entrance, compositions to pick up the theme and look of a new exhibition, seasonal decorations, and special requests.

Art in Bloom at Home presents the wisdom accumulated during these activities by several generations of Ladies Committee members. I hope this book will help you create arrangements for your home that are as lovely as those that grace the Museum of Fine Arts. Your flowers, whether meant for the coffee table, the front hall console, or the dining room, should bring you as much pleasure as we derive from arrangements that are placed beside Museum masterpieces.

The book begins with styles of arrangements, moves to rules for design, and then goes on to such practical considerations as materials, containers, mechanics, care, and a section of "recipes" that will guide you through the creation of your own arrangements. The book ends with specific conditioning for more than three hundred cut plant varieties. All materials discussed in this book are readily available from local nurseries, florists, garden club plant sales, or from your own garden.

Notes

Introduction

Flower arranging relies upon both art and nature. Nature provides the materials, but how we select and organize these materials to create a composition that has appropriate form, texture, and color is an art. Placing a single bloom or a small bouquet in a vase calls attention to the beauty of nature, while organizing the same material into a design can produce a work of art.

The principles of design that shape the creation of all art remain the same regardless of the medium an artist chooses to work in -- they are *proportion, scale, balance, rhythm, dominance* and *contrast.* To adhere to these principles, the flower arranger uses the eight elements of design -- space, light, color, form, texture, size, line and pattern. Throughout the text, the principles appear in italics to underscore how use of the eight elements helps the arranger to develop a good design.

Design is always first and foremost! The folding camp chair used today by visitors to the Museum was actually designed for Tutankhamen in 1500 BC. Although King Tut's stool certainly was more elaborate and decorative, it is the design that has survived.

My plan is to fortify you with all pertinent information so that, as you begin the chapter on Creating Arrangements, you will understand how and why the "recipes" in that section produce successful designs.

Appendix C lists special conditioning treatments for over 300 flowers. Proper conditioning is paramount for your success.

Notes

Design for Flower Arranging

Styles of Flower Design

Traditional styles of floral arrangement take the form of mass design, line design, or line-mass design. No matter which form your design takes, the key to success is that it must have visual stability, or *balance*. The design may be symmetrical or asymmetrical, but unless it gives the impression of being stable it will disturb the viewer.

To be *balanced*, your design must allow for equal visual weight in the distribution of elements around the axis, an imaginary vertical line that runs through the visual center of gravity of your arrangement.

Arranging on a lazy Susan, so that you view your work not only from the front and back but also from the right and left, will help you achieve *balance* and avoid the beginner's most common mistake — putting most of the flowers in the front. Note how the arrangement (Fig. 1) viewed from the side appears to tip forward. With the addition of one bud, one leaf, and one fully opened bloom in the back, the design gains depth and stability.

Fig. 1   1.   2.

Fig. 1. To create depth, place your flowers at different heights and do not line them up on a horizontal plane.

11

Mass Design

Mass design achieves symmetrical *balance* by the repetition of all elements on each side of the vertical axis, xx, (Fig. 2). The visual center of gravity ▲, is generally on this axis, slightly below the center of the design, as measured from the extreme bottom of the composition (container, accessories, and flowers) to the extreme top. The eye goes directly to this spot; this is your point of *dominance*. Put weight here with color, form, or texture, as well as size.

Mass designs are closed forms, such as cones, cylinders or spheres; they require large quantities of flowers and foliage, but they should not be over-stuffed! The Japanese say "Allow enough room for the butterfly to pass through."

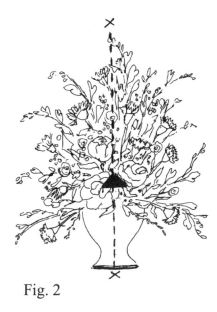

Fig. 2

Fig. 2. Mass symmetrical; stems should seem to emerge from a central point, as they would on a growing plant.

Line Design

Line design is an open form, characterized by use of minimal materials with a strong line, in the manner of Ikebana, the Japanese art of flower arranging (Fig. 3). A line design must have only one focal point, and this *dominance* ▲ should be at the rim of the container, on the axis, xx.

The line may be straight or curved, symmetrical or asymmetrical, but it will be obvious and it will have *balance*. Think about the teeter-totter you played on as a child. Your friend was smaller, so you had to move closer to the fulcrum to balance her weight. Just so, in your arrangement, larger, heavier forms must be placed close to the fulcrum or axis; however, in a line design, the axis will not necessarily be at the center of the container.

Line-mass Design

Line-mass design (Fig. 4) combines the two previous styles. It is an open form that uses more material than a line design. The line may be straight or curved, but a definite, well planned linear pattern with *dominance* on the axis, xx, creating interest, is paramount to the *balance* of the design and to its aesthetic beauty.

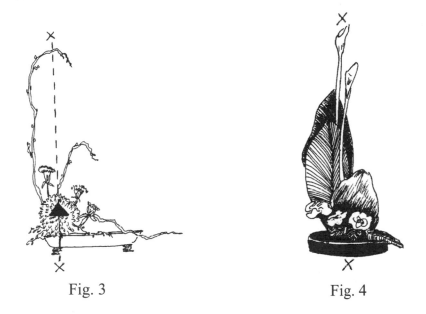

Fig. 3   Fig. 4

Fig. 3. Line asymmetrical; dominance is created by massing the largest and brightest forms at the rim of the container.

Fig. 4. Line-Mass asymmetrical; actual material placed to left of the axis balances the visual weight that occurs naturally on the right. The color, texture and overlapping of forms and their proportions create a visual path.

13

Space

Space is your first consideration in planning a floral arrangement. Your design must be appropriate in *scale*, or size, to the area in which it will be placed. The space you work with includes the size of the room, other objects within view, the distance from which the arrangement will be seen, and the illumination within the room. Like an artist staring at a blank canvas, you need to develop a concept that is in *proportion* to that space.

Where will your design be placed?

- Against a wall? An arrangement on the fireplace mantel shelf will be viewed only from the front, the right side, and the left side, but it must still work with its surroundings (Fig. 5).

Fig. 5

Fig. 5. All objects and open areas in your design are important to the composition.

14

- Free standing? An arrangement on a coffee table will be viewed in the round, so all sides must be finished and *balanced*.

At what distance will your design be seen?

- Far from the viewer, as in a great hall or a church? Something like a Magnolia branch might be right for *scale.*

- On the dining table? This is the perfect place to appreciate small, delicate forms, such as Sweet Peas and Lilies-of-the-valley.

Space also exists within your design. Voids between the lines and forms of plant material are as important as solid areas. They are restful and make the solid material more important. (Note the voids between the candles and the plant material in Fig. 5.) Interesting spaces also help to achieve an uncluttered effect. The most common fault wc scc in arrangements is the use of too much material. Blank spaces and solids should *balance* as you develop your design.

If you have seven beautiful Roses, but only five are needed for your pattern, save those two extra Roses for bud vases in the bath and kitchen. Don't overstuff. Stand back and view your design. Will the butterfly find room to hover?

Light

The importance of light lies in its effect on color. As Monet's grainstack series demonstrates, changes in light produce great variation in the appearance of color. Intense, natural light from overhead, such as from the sun at midday, reveals what we think of as the actual color of a flower — i.e., its brightest appearance. However, most floral designs are created for indoor lighting conditions — incandescent and fluorescent, both of which differ very much from daylight.

The more intense the light, the brighter and truer your colors will appear. Conversely, at low levels of light, materials darken; in particular, green material becomes blue, and blue and purple disappear. So, if you are creating an arrangement for a low-light situation, such as an evening reception, be careful with these colors.

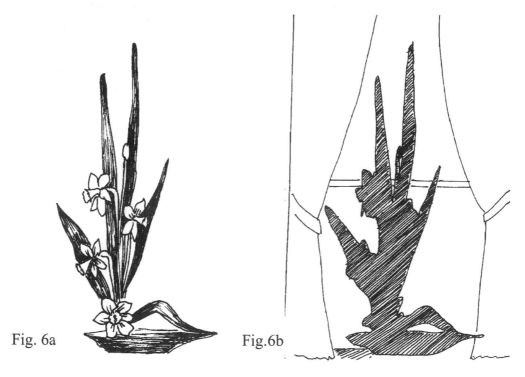

Fig. 6a   Fig.6b

Fig. 6a. Light coming from all directions at once will not distort your design.

Fig. 6b. Light coming through an arrangement, as from a window, reacts with your material.

Light that comes from behind severely affects your design (Fig 6b). When an arrangement is placed in front of a window, for example, the light produces a silhouette effect. Colors appear weaker and duller, and the background seems annoyingly bright in contrast to the flowers. On the other hand, light from a source in front of and above a design will produce shadows that can be incorporated into the design (Fig. 6c). Arrangers at Art in Bloom usually try to achieve this effect when the object being interpreted is either a statue that casts its own shadow or a painting that includes a prominent shadow within its design.

Because the kind, the amount, and the direction of light can make dramatic changes in the appearance of your arrangement, you should always try to design in the same light and space in which your arrangement will be viewed. Also keep in mind that light produces heat. Too much light, whether from the sun or from a bulb, will wilt your flowers.

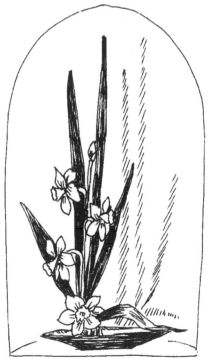

Fig. 6c

Fig. 6c. Light coming from in front of your arrangement producing shadows can add a new dimension to your design.

17

Color

Good design does not require color. In some cases, color may even deceive your eye as you work. Therefore, since a floral designer does not have the option of working only in black and white, one needs to develop a good understanding of how color affects what we see.

To begin with, color is defined by *hue* — i.e., its specific name, like red, blue, or yellow. Variations in the *value* of a hue occur when white is added to make a tint, such as pink, or when black is added to create a shade, such as burgundy. *Saturation*, the brightness or dullness of a color, is greatly affected by the intensity of the hue itself and the texture of the surface. Completely described, the color of a Daffodil is light, bright yellow; the color of an Oak leaf is dark, dull green.

Colors are also referred to as warm — red, yellow, orange, or cool — blue, green, purple. The lighter, brighter, and warmer a color is, the more it will *dominate*. Use hues of this kind to design for large spaces. In every arrangement, place your *dominant* colors low and toward the center of your design to provide weight and *balance*. The darker, duller, and cooler a color is, the more it will recede. Use these hues to provide *rhythm* and *contrast*.

Color reacts with adjacent colors in very interesting ways. Complementary colors, those opposite one another on the color wheel, can give a sense of excitement to your arrangement, provided they have the same value and saturation. Red and green, blue and orange are complementary combinations. Therefore, bright orange Carnations used with bright red Gladiolus will appear even brighter when used with complementary blue-green or very dull foliage. Purple and yellow are also complementary, but their values and saturation are so different that using them together can create a spotty effect with divided *dominance* which can disturb balance.

Rarely is a color pure. Be sure to examine your materials carefully to determine what mix of hues they are. Check a color wheel to find combinations that work. For example, light, bright pink Nerines will appear more intense next to light, dull Bells-of-Ireland, because the yellow-green of Bells-of-Ireland is directly opposite on the color wheel to the blue-pink of Nerines.

The greater the *contrast* the more *dominant* are the colors we see. Black with white is definitely more vibrant than gray with white. Related hues, such as light, bright, yellow Roses with the dull brown undersides of Magnolia leaves can also provide interesting *contrast*. A gradual change in color, on the other hand, moving outward from the center to the edges of your arrangement, will produce a pleasing *rhythm* in your design.

Viewing your design as a black and white photograph (Fig. 7) will reveal the correct use of advancing and receding color. You will be able to see any interruptions in *rhythm*, as well as voids.

Fig. 7

Fig. 7. Correct placement of receding hues creates rhythm in this design.

Form

Form is three dimensional; it can be closed or open, round or spike-like. Because it is a closed form, a Dahlia will appear heavier than an open-form Iris of the same size (Fig. 8a). Thus, the Dahlia is visually more *dominant*. Similarly, the round, closed form of a Rose will dominate the spike-like form of a Snapdragon.

Dominant forms, as well as *dominant* colors, belong low and toward the center of your design. If you are working with small flowers, such as mini Carnations, you can create a closed and *dominant* form by grouping many stems together (Fig. 8b).

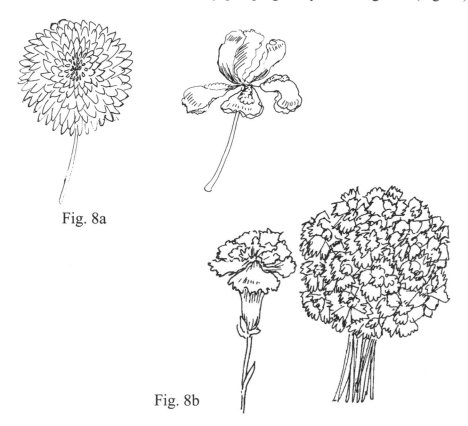

Fig. 8a

Fig. 8b

Fig. 8a. Keep closed, dominant forms low and toward the center of your arrangement.

Fig. 8b. Grouping stems can create dominance, while scattering the same flowers may cause a spotty effect.

Going in the other direction, you may prune leaves and flowers to make them lighter forms. Even though a branch may be lush with foliage, your design may require you to do some judicious thinning (Figs. 9a & b).

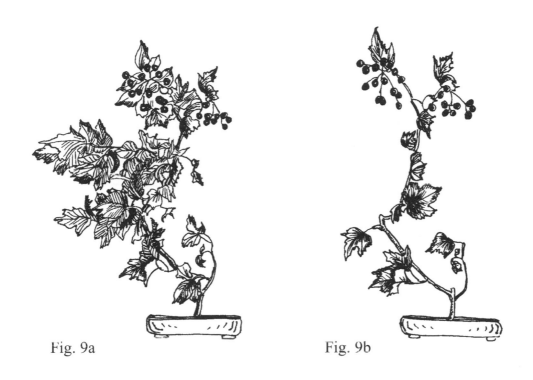

Fig. 9a   Fig. 9b

Fig. 9. Pruning clarifies the line of design, creating direction and making space for complementary materials.

Forms themselves must be harmonious in *scale*. For example, Hosta, Leucothoe, and Peony work well together. If you substitute Bridal Wreath for Leucothoe, however, the *scale* of the Bridal Wreath will be too fine for the Hosta and Peony. Such substitution would create too much *contrast*, causing a loss of *balance*.

Flat shapes, such as leaves, also provide *rhythm*. They allow the eye to move through the design, not only because of the tranquillity of their form but also because of the neutrality of the color green.

21

Texture

The surfaces of flowers, leaves, branches, and containers used in your design may be glossy or dull, smooth or rough, coarse or fine. Glossy surfaces reflect more light than dull surfaces, thereby making material appear larger and colors appear brighter. Glossy textures are therefore *dominant*. Because of its surface, a glossy white Anthurium will seem larger and brighter than a dull white Calla Lily of the same size.

In like manner, the smooth surface of a Hosta leaf will *dominate* the fuzzy surface of a Begonia leaf, although they both may be the same color and size. Similarly, bold textures seem heavier than fine textures. A stem of Rhododendron will visually outweigh and *dominate* the finer stem of a Fern (Figs. 10a&b).

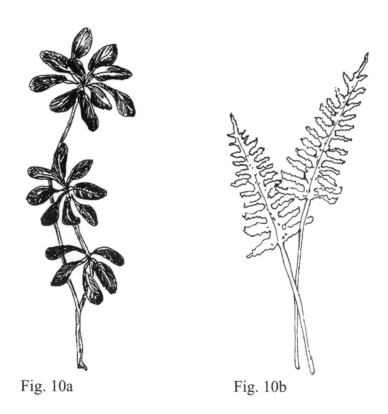

Fig. 10a   Fig. 10b

Fig. 10a. Bold textures are dramatic and easier to see from a distance.

Fig. 10b. Fine textures invite closer examination.

The textures of your container and the pebbles, mosses, or leaves that cover your mechanics play a major role in the overall effect produced by your design. This is an especially important point to keep in mind, when you use *contrasting* textures to provide *rhythm* in your arrangement. An excellent example at the MFA of the use of such contrast is the *Bartlett Head of Aphrodite*. Carved from fine-grained Parian marble, this portrait of the Greek goddess of love and beauty gains much of its appeal from the contrast in texture between her very smooth cheek and the rough locks of her elaborate hairdo.

Size

The perceived size, or visual weight, of flowers and greens is affected by the elements that have already been discussed — space, color, texture and form. The greater the distance from the viewer, the smaller an object will appear. Blue and violet objects appear smaller than white and yellow colors. Coarse and dull textures appear smaller than smooth, shiny textures. Open forms, such as field Daisies, appear smaller than such closed, solid forms as Zinnias.

On the other hand, the visual weight of each flower or leaf increases the farther it moves away from the central axis — similar to *balancing* your weight on a teeter-totter. To develop an understanding of this visual *balance*, simply follow Nature (Fig. 11). As you move away from the center of your arrangement, the visual weight of your material should move from large to small.

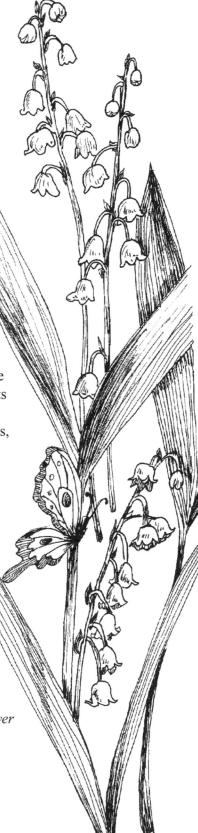

Fig. 11

Fig. 11. A stem of flowers is good design, because the opened flower at the bottom is larger than the bud at the top.

Line

Line is the primary foundation, the skeleton of your design. It may be straight or curved, but it creates a visual path, motion, or *rhythm* that leads the eye from one point of interest to another. These points of interest are produced by flowers, leaves, and branches. Think of line as the melody moving throughout a symphony, and of color, form, and texture as the instruments that make the score complete.

Be aware of how your line affects the viewer. For example, a diagonal straight line can be dramatic (Fig.12). A vertical straight line tends to be inspirational and is very appropriate for an altarpiece; a horizontal straight line conveys a feeling of tranquillity, such as is wanted at a dinner table. A successful combination of the two — one vertical and one horizontal — produces an asymmetrical L line design that strongly directs the eye (Fig. 13).

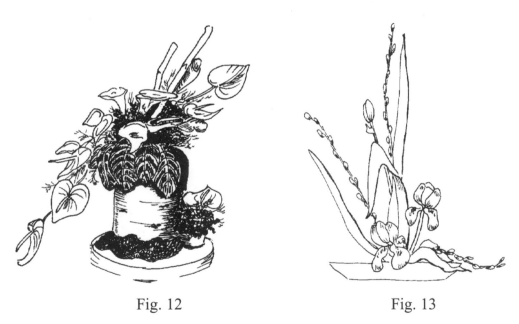

Fig. 12   Fig. 13

Fig. 12. In this diagonal line-mass arrangement, the strong cylindrical pattern comes from the use of bold floral forms in correct proportions..

Fig. 13. For an L design, putting the axis of your arrangement on the left and leaving open space to the right will create the impression of stability, or balance.

A curved line may be a semi-circle in a perfectly symmetrical position or a crescent lying on its side. In this latter position, the upper portion of a crescent, that part of the line above the rim of the container, should be longer than the lower part and should direct the eye (Fig. 14). A serpentine or Hogarth curve is a combination of two semi-circles. *Dominance* results at the center, where the two semi-circles meet. Again, the line of the upper curve should be longer than that of the lower reverse curve.

Whatever you use to establish your line, flowers, leaves, or branches, keep in mind that each piece of plant material has naturally flowing outlines. Good design incorporates this inherent grace through careful placement of each component. Good design also moves from solidity to airiness. You should try to reinforce your established line through repetition of shape, form, size, color, or texture moving in a linear direction — e.g., red at the center moving to pink at the extremities or a large round form at the center moving outward to smaller round forms of the same material.

Fig. 14

Fig. 14. Varying the direction of the.Llilies gives this crescent depth.

25

Pattern

Line and pattern are closely related. Line, which is two-dimensional and skeletal, helps to establish pattern, which is three-dimensional and fully developed. Pattern arises from the combination of plant material, container, and accessories. It is composed of lines, textures, forms, colors, and the spaces between them. It is what gives depth, interest, and feeling to your arrangement. The pattern may take the form of a cone, a cylinder or a sphere.

Creating a successful pattern requires a minimum of three varieties of flower or foliage. You might start with two flowers plus one foliage — Lilacs and Tulips with Lilac leaves; or one flower with two greens — Iris, Iris leaves, and Willow; or three varieties of greens. Remember to *contrast* form, texture, and color and to keep all components in *scale*.

Fig. 15

Fig. 15. Overlapping forms provide contrast and rhythm. The use of flowers, leaves and branches are in scale and provide a pattern with form, texture and color.

Your goal should be an interesting silhouette with relative areas of solids and voids. It is helpful to think of all material as coming from one point, as a plant would grow (Fig. 16a). Crossed lines (Fig. 16b) disturb your viewer, because they interfere with this natural *rhythm*.

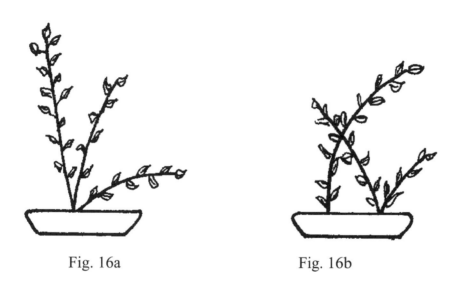

Fig. 16a   Fig. 16b

Fig. 16a. When material comes from a central spot, the eye follows it naturally upward from the base.

Fig. 16b. Crossed lines direct the eye in different directions without focus.

When you start to create a design, you should develop a mental image of your pattern, so that you can select your materials. Look at your space, look at your container, and look at your flowers and foliage or branch material. Flowers, leaves, and stems have size, weight, form, texture, direction and color, all of which contribute to pattern. As you place each stem, consider the voids. If a stem interferes, remove it. Determine your pattern and stick to it!

Getting Started

Selecting Material

As you practice the eight elements of design, your confidence in your own judgment will build. You will find it easier to select material for a flower arrangement. For now, it is important to note that the materials you choose must be appropriate for the space, the season of the year, and the mood of the occasion.

For example, an arrangement for a dining table should be no more than 14" high, so that people seated at the table can see over the flowers. For this space, plan a low, horizontal pattern in colors that are compatible with your china and linens. Conversely, a large hall may require a 6'-8' design with large forms and warm, advancing hues that will catch the attention of a distant viewer.

The Right Flower

Materials appropriate to the season are easy to identify. In spring, for example, use pastel hues, such as those found in Crocus and Pussy Willow, light green foliage, yellow Daffodils, pink Tulips, flowering fruit trees, and Azalea. Coral Bells, beardless Iris, and Bleeding Hearts will work well together for a springtime coffee table arrangement, while Poinsettia would be completely out of place.

For summer, bright hues, such as those found in blue Delphiniums, yellow Marigolds, and red Zinnias are appropriate, while needled evergreens just won't work. White and green in a variety of textures and forms are cooling on a hot August afternoon.

In autumn, Chrysanthemums, Sedums, and Safflower in russet/orange shades, Hydrangea and Sourwood in elegant burgundies, along with Dahlias in many hues give us a last surge of color. At this time of year summer or spring flowers like Lilacs and Tulips, even though available commercially, are not timely in a design.

Winter is the time for a wonderful mix of red and green. Red Carnations and bright pink Nerines combined with deep green Yew look like winter. So do bare branches; their interesting lines can produce a fascinating winter silhouette. Toward the end of winter, watch for early blooming Witch Hazel, easily overlooked against the drab winter landscape. This harbinger of spring brings us full circle through the year.

From among nature's seasonal offerings, try to pick materials that are appropriate for the occasion. Violet and blue produce a tranquil atmosphere appropriate for a ladies' lunch. Roses and Lilies are elegant, formal flowers; use these for weddings. Hues of bright red, blue, and green, which seem to signify strength and vitality, are excellent choices to celebrate holidays, graduations, or promotions. Bright yellow, hot pink, and lime green express joy and would be perfect for a baby shower, while light lavender Lilacs, Lady's Mantle, and Bridal Wreath imply gentleness and are just right for a bridal shower.

Most men like red and russet hues. Try red Gladiolus and orange Carnations with strong foliage, such as Lemon Leaf or Leucothoe for your husband's birthday. But even though the colors may be right, never use red Roses and orange Nasturtiums together, because they *contrast* too much in form.

Forcing

In winter, you may also want to try forcing some branches into early bloom. The closer to the time of natural bloom a branch is forced, the sooner its flowers or leaves will appear. Azalea, Crabapple, Dogwood, Forsythia, flowering Plum, Redbud and Witch Hazel are excellent candidates for forcing. (Fig. 17). First, submerge the entire branch under water for at least one hour (or wait to cut on a warm, rainy day in January or February). Next, since this is woody material, crush the stem's cut end, or crosscut it vertically and peel the bark back 2". Immediately place the cut stem into very hot water to which you have added aspirin, vinegar or a commercial preservative. Use water as hot as it comes out of the tap. Your branch may take days or weeks to force, and the preservative will discourage bacteria from growing. Use only enough water to cover the cut and exposed area of the stem, so there will be room to add hot water daily. Mist daily and keep the branch in a warm, sunny location. You are trying to make the branch think it is spring!

Fig. 17

Fig. 17. A branch that is no longer than three feet will be easier to force.

Other Concerns

Some additional considerations are in order:

- Choose colors, forms, and textures to complement your container and to develop your pattern. Especially lovely is a copper container filled with Winterberry, Umbrella Pine, and Pieris japonica.
- Using an uneven number of like material — say, five Iris instead of four — generally produces a more interesting design. For example, when faced with the problem of painting a portrait of four young girls (*The Daughters of Edward D. Boit*), John Singer Sargent grouped the two older girls toward the back to create only three dominant areas of white apron and placed a doll in the youngest's arms to make five faces, or forms, rather than four.
- When you can, enjoy nature and use materials from the garden. No matter what the season, a florist's material can sometimes be too perfect and uniform. Flowers and greens from the garden can offer more graceful, natural lines. A bare branch from a fruit tree, if carefully pruned, can become a very creative line design.
- Look at the stems of flowers and branch material to determine how they grew. If you have planned your design to direct the eye to the left, then gather line material that grew in that direction. If you have not determined your line and are looking for inspiration, let nature be your guide. A deformed growth on a plant can produce a very creative design. Fasciated Willow and Harry Lauder's Walking Stick are whimsical materials that can be used with minimal reinforcement, as their lines are interesting in and of themselves (Fig. 18).

Fig. 18

Fig. 18. The interesting design created by this branch could be enhanced by the addition of one large Chrysanthemum at the base.

- Don't overlook the appeal of foliage from house plants. Spathiphyllum, Chinese Evergreen, all Philodendrons, and Ficus lyrata (large fiddle-shaped leaves) are a few that come to mind.
- When you must purchase flowers, look at their leaves. Are they yellowing or wilted? If so, they are too old, even if the flowers themselves look happy. Gently shake the stems to see if any petals drop. Be aware that flower prices are much higher at holidays, especially on St. Valentine's Day.
- Be aware that fruits and some flowers simply don't get along together. A few varieties of Orchid, for example, emit a gas that harms Carnations, Lilies, and Snapdragons but doesn't bother Roses, Dendrobiums, and Oncidiums. If you combine Apples and Holly, the Holly will shrivel overnight. In like fashion, Bananas will destroy Lilies.
- Be aware of how your material smells. Floral scents can compete with food aromas. Gypsophila, Eucalyptus and Genista, if used in quantity, can create an unpleasant odor. Gardenias and Casa Blanca Lilies have a heavy perfume better suited to a bridal bouquet than a dining table.

Other Sources

Look beyond the garden and the florist:
- Become familiar with wild flowers. Queen Anne's Lace, Yarrow, wild Aster, Rose hips, Tansy, Goldenrod and Dock are a few favorites. (The old myth that Goldenrod causes hayfever is not true. It blooms at the same time as Ragweed, which does have pollen that produces hayfever, but the yellow of the Goldenrod is what people see and accuse.) Before you cut, however, know which plants are on the protected list for the state in which you are cutting.
- Observe nature in different seasons. Dock, for instance, changes color as summer advances, from green to pink to brown.

- Look in the forest for Mosses, Lichens and Cones that you can use at the base of your arrangement. Collect Moss that grows on rocks, because Moss from fallen trees can be very buggy. Lichen that grows on fallen Birch lasts well and dries firm, but it will soften and decay if allowed to get wet. It is a good idea to put the material you collect into a plastic bag, give it a generous spray of insect killer, and seal the bag for at least one hour.
- Search the shoreline for interesting shells, driftwood and rocks to use as containers for your designs (Fig. 19).
- Finally, don't overlook fruits and vegetables. Their beautiful colors, forms and textures have inspired many excellent Williamsburg designs.

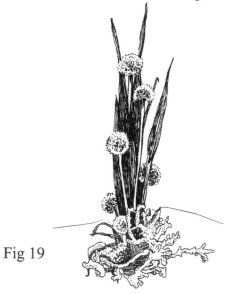

Fig 19

Fig. 19. A piece of Coral camouflages the pin holder in this arrangement.

Cutting Time and Tools

Water is the staff of life for flowers. When a stem is cut from a growing plant, it loses its source of moisture and suffers immediate evaporation from its leaves and flowers. Some flowers can last only three hours after a cut. For this reason, when you are collecting material from the garden, it is important to take along a bucket of water in which to place the stems. Even having taken this precaution, no amount of conditioning or care will restore a flower that has been cut at the wrong time or in the wrong way.

The worst time to cut is in the middle of a sunny day, because plant chemistry is most active in sunshine. Your material will do much better if you cut it early in the morning, before the dew is off the bloom, or after the sun has gone down when plants have recovered from the heat of the day. Really, the ideal time to cut is on a rainy morning, when metabolism is low and cells are filled with moisture.

Try to cut flowers just before they reach their prime — i.e., before the pollen is fully developed. (Exceptions to this rule are covered in Appendix C.) On the other hand, the foliage you select should be mature and hardened. Avoid new spring growth, as it will wilt. If your foliage has new growth at the tip, remove it.

Before cutting, fill a clean, plastic bucket 1/3 full with water that is slightly cooler than the surrounding air. Place cut stems into the water immediately, taking care not to crowd them. Soiled buckets harbor bacteria that will destroy your flowers. Plastic is preferred, because the edges of metal buckets can damage stems, and the metal itself may react chemically with your additives.

As you cut, be mindful of the health of the plant. Cut a stem just above a leaf node (where a leaf joins the stem). A Rose stem, for example, should be cut just above a five leaflet node. This type of cut will encourage the plant to continue producing new growth.

Keep a clean, sharp tool, such as a knife, scissors, or clippers with sharp blades on both sides, for cutting plant material and use it only for this purpose. Never use blade-and-anvil tools or dull kitchen shears; they will crush or otherwise damage the cells of a stem. Cut each stem on a slant to expose as large a surface as possible for water absorption. It is easier to cut a thick branch by pointing the clippers downward toward the root system.

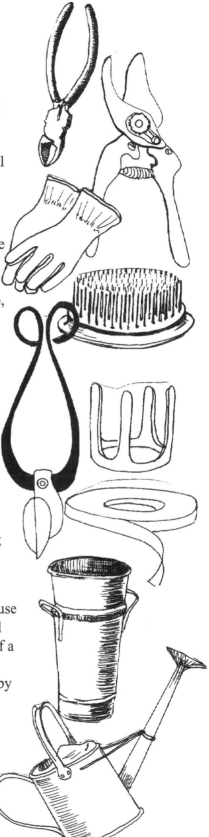

Conditioning

Conditioning, or hydrating, is the process of encouraging water to flow up into the cut plant material. To begin the conditioning process, fill clean plastic buckets with clean water of appropriate temperatures to a depth sufficient to cover at least 1" above the cut. The number of buckets you will need depends on the assortment of materials that you have cut or purchased, as explained below.

For **all** materials, follow these general guidelines:

- Remove all leaves from flower stems, except in certain cases discussed in Appendix C. You want the water to travel directly up to the flower head as soon as possible and not to migrate into each leaf.
- Cut separate leaf stems for use as foliage. Woody branches obviously are cut for their foliage, and so you should remove leaves only from the section of branch that will be under water.
- Cut stems on a slant to expose as much surface as possible to the water.
- Keep stems reasonably long; you can do very little with too short a stem. A reasonable cut would be not much longer than you need for your design; the shorter the distance the water must travel the less stress the flower must endure.
- Cut materials under water to prevent air bubbles that will block water flow up the stems.
- Quickly transfer material into buckets with the proper water temperature and hold at room temperature for one hour.
- Move the buckets for overnight to a cool dark area — if possible, to an area that is free of air circulation and has temperatures of 40-45 degrees. Flowers can take from 6 to 24 hours to hydrate, depending on how they were treated between the time they were cut and the time you began to condition them.

34

- Do not condition in an automatic defrosting refrigerator, because it circulates air that will dry your flower petals.
- Handle flowers as little as possible. Flower petals are very delicate, and touching bruises their flesh. For the same reason, do not crowd flowers in your conditioning buckets.
- Mist material frequently during conditioning.
- After each use, wash your conditioning and collecting buckets with detergent and disinfect with bleach, so they will be free of bacteria for the next time.

The character of the stem determines the **temperature** of the conditioning water:
- Put soft stems, such as Tulips, Snapdragons, Lily-of-the-valley and most wild flowers, into water slightly cooler than body temperature — but never below 80° F.
- Put woody stems, such as Chrysanthemums, Peonies and Astilbe, into lukewarm water, about 95-100° F.
- Put woody branches, such as Azalea, Viburnum and Cherry, into warm water, 110-120° F.

The character of the stem also determines the **treatment** of the cut:
- Either crush a woody branch or cross-cut it vertically on the cut end to expose more area to moisture. If possible, peel back 1"-2" of outer dead bark to expose the green cambium that carries nutrients to the leaves. The more of this area you expose to warm water, the longer your branch will remain fresh.
- Seal any stem that exudes a milky substance by burning or boiling the tip, so that the substance cannot foul the water. Killing the cells in the bottoms of the stems slows dehydration in Gerbera and Dahlias and stops the flow of the milky substance produced by Euphorbias, such as Poinsettia and Snow-on-the-Mountain. For an effective seal, either submerge the tip under about 1/4" of boiling water or burn it with a flame for about 30 seconds; then, place in conditioning water of the correct temperature. (Be sure to protect flowers from the heat.)
- Tulips, Daffodils, and other flowers that grow from a bulb are often cut to include the white part at the bottom of the stem; remove this white section, because water travels up only the green part of the stem.

- Submerge material with a smooth surface, such as Hosta and leafy branches, or with multiple loose clusters, such as Lilac, Hydrangea, many wild flowers and Fern, in cool water for at least one hour to as long as over night. An extra bath tub is handy, but Lilacs, for example, can be carefully placed head down in a bucket of water and then re-cut. (Never wet furry leaves, such as African Violets or Lamb's Ears; they will mildew.)
- Do not refrigerate Anthurium, Bird of Paradise, Camellia, Ginger, Heliconia, or any other flower that grows in a warm climate. Keep them away from drafts and extremes in temperature.
- Hollow-stemmed flowers, such as Larkspur, Lupine and Water Lilies, are just begging for water to reach their flower heads. Turn these flowers upside down, and fill their stems with an eyedropper. Plug each stem with cotton, wax, or floral foam, and carefully place it in conditioning water. (Although tedious, this process, like sealing, is well worth your trouble, because it significantly extends the vase life of your flowers.)
- Condition Daffodils, Asters, Marigolds, Zinnias and Gypsophila in separate buckets, because they tend to foul the water while hydrating.

Special treatments in your conditioning and arranging water will prolong the life of your floral material by providing food, killing or restricting bacteria, reducing gas production and improving acidity levels. The easiest way to start is with commercial products, which are mixed in proper percentages and are safe for most flowers. However, if you wish to make your own, here are some useful **additives**:
- Alcohol: One-half teaspoon of grain alcohol, never rubbing alcohol, in one quart of conditioning water helps keep stems rigid and straight, especially Tulips, Wisteria and Clematis.

36

- Aspirin: Dissolving aspirin in water increases its acidity; acidic solutions move into stems more readily than neutral or alkaline solutions and they also restrict bacterial growth.
- Bleach: Some arrangers condition in a chlorine solution to inhibit bacterial growth; this practice is questionable. Chlorine does kill bacteria, but it kills plant tissue as well. One benefit, however, is that it discourages odor from Alliums.
- Fixative spray: Application retards evaporation of moisture from a flower head; use in low humidity and especially for tropical flowers, such as Heliconia and Ginger, and for multi-blossomed flower heads, such as Lilac.
- Sugar: One teaspoon of sugar in one quart of water provides nourishment.
- Vinegar: One teaspoon of vinegar in one quart of water increases acidity, which aids in water uptake and thus lengthens the vase life of many flowers.

Another special case of flower treatment is to speed the opening of buds or to encourage a purchased or cut flower to full bloom. First, rinse buds under lukewarm water and condition in warm to hot water to which you have added sugar. Mist frequently, and do not refrigerate. Carnations, Gladiolus, Roses, Protea and Chrysanthemums respond well to this treatment. If Rose buds have dry outside petals, peel them back. Gently break the seals between Lily petals with your fingers.

If you must transport stems without water, condition them overnight, place the cut stem-ends in a plastic bag, and tie securely to seal in moisture. Delicate flowers, such as Roses or Lily-of-the-valley, should never be without water and must therefore be put into water picks.

Most significant is the fact that proper conditioning can extend the life of most designs so that they can remain fresh for many days.

Containers

Your choice of container is a very important decision. Anything that holds water can be a container, but it must integrate into your design. To work together well, container and flowers must be in *proportion* to each other — a matter of size and shape — and they must be compatible in color and texture.

The size and shape of a container determine the *scale* and *pattern* of your finished arrangement. Consider the opening; the larger it is, the more material you need. Even a small Paul Revere bowl requires a mass design and, consequently, a large quantity of flowers. A large, tall urn, on the other hand, may not have an opening big enough to accommodate as much heavy material as you had planned. Calla Lily and Anthurium stems, for example, require a lot of room. Large branches and heavy flowers, such as Peonies, also need depth to support their weight.

Consider the shape; a massive vase requires material higher or wider than itself, or the container will *dominate* the scene. If flower height should happen to be less than urn height, you must increase the spread of your design to achieve *proportion* and *balance*.

A flat dish works beautifully with a line design created in a kenzan, or pin holder. A delicate pitcher with painted wild flowers requires finer, smaller flowers than does a ceramic crock. If a basket is your container, you may choose to use, ignore, or hide the handle. If it is to remain visible, then keep your material clear, so the handle may be easily grasped.

38

As you select your container, think about its color and texture. It's color must blend with your materials. Brass, for example, works with materials that tend toward the yellow hues, while copper blends with hues in the red family. Porcelain and pottery have their own colors, at least one of which should be repeated in your flowers

Alabaster and bronze are ideal, because they are neutral in both color and texture. Glossy white or polished silver, however, is so *dominant*, that it can easily *unbalance* your design. (If you must use grandmother's milk glass pitcher, be sure to include some yellow and white flowers with variegated foliage to blend with and offset the dominant white of the container.)

The textures of container and materials must also be compatible. A basket made of dull brown rushes and filled with glossy dark green European Ginger is a marriage, whereas it takes fuzzy grey Lamb's Ears to do justice to an antique black iron pot. This is an area of design with which you should have fun experimenting.

Not so much fun is glass, which can pose a major challenge. In general, glass containers are more trouble than they're worth. Arrangement of the stems under water becomes as important to your design as the flowers above; you must, for the sake of cleanliness, change rather than add water, and so on. My advice is to save these containers for bouquets, rather than try to use them in a design.

Sometimes what you envision as a great container just won't hold water. Not to worry. If you don't have anything on hand that will work well with the available plant material, use your imagination:

- Liners can turn almost anything into a container. You can buy liners in many shapes or save used plastic food cartons and water bottles. If necessary, you can add stones or sand for stability.
- Vases and bowls are obvious containers, but a piece of driftwood or a seashell could help you make a stunning design. Conceal a pin holder within, and flowers and container seem to be an organic whole.
- Make an interesting container by using Moss to cover a floral foam brick sealed in plastic. The brick itself will not leak, but to be completely safe, you can use a tray under your arrangement. (Moss acts like a wick and may create puddles at the edges.)

- Paint any waterproof tin or plastic a dark, dull color and cover it with sheet Moss. Work with large sheets, arranging them carefully. Have a friend hold the Moss in place, while you slip an elastic or two around it. When you are satisfied, secure the Moss with raffia or green florist's string and remove the elastic by cutting. Moss can also be glued in place with a glue gun or floral glue.
- Sculpt some chicken wire into any shape you want — a duck, a sphere, free-form — and then paint it green. Leave an opening so you can line your sculpture with sheet Moss and fill it with floral foam or soil, depending on whether you want to pin flowers to it or insert a plant.
- Use styrofoam cones and spheres as bases for fruit, silk and dried arrangements. For example, to make a "Williamsburg" Apple and fruit tree, impale the fruit on wooden skewers and insert them into a cone. (If your cone is white, paint it first using a floral paint that will not dissolve plastic.) If you preserve the fruit with an acrylic spray, your tree can last for weeks; just keep it in a cool place when it is not on display.

As you can see, the possibilities are endless. If your imagination needs jogging, look at what other people do. At Art in Bloom each year, containers are as much talked about as flowers. There is always enough inspiration at this event for a whole year of new ideas.

Mechanics

The word mechanics describes any thing you use to hold your design together. Fortunately, several commercial solutions have been developed to keep a stem in place. Some of them have already been mentioned in the section above. What follows is an alphabetical list of mechanics that you will begin collecting, as you work your way through the section on Creating Arrangements. By familiarizing yourself with the terms here, you'll know what is wanted for each of the designs you attempt. In Appendix B, you'll find a more extensive list of supplies.

- **Anchor Pins** (Fig. 20) are used to hold a brick of floral foam securely in a shallow container.

Fig.20

Fig. 20. Use floral clay to attach an anchor pin to the bottom of your container.

- **Chicken Wire** comes in a 1" grid and is used over floral foam to keep heavy materials stable and to prevent foam from crumbling. To use, cut a piece of wire slightly larger than the opening of your container and bend it over the foam, tucking the ends in (Fig. 21). You may want to spray it with moss green or brown paint, so that the wire will not shine through.

Fig. 21

Fig. 21. Be careful not to scratch your container with wire; use a liner

- **Dry Floral Foam**, which is available in brown bricks, does not absorb water; it is used with dried or silk materials. Sculpt it to fit your container or use it for a design without a container, such as silk flowers for the mantelpiece.
- **Elastics** are useful for attaching flowers to such objects as chandeliers or church pews.

- The **Floral Adhesive** developed by the Smithers Company will not damage fresh flowers. This product makes it possible to glue flowers, out of water, wherever you want them — Orchids spilling down the sides of a moss-covered container, Galax leaves covering a glass bowl, Freesia and European Ginger leaves made into a bobeche for your candelabra. Be sure to use well conditioned materials and expect the flower to have a shorter life than when it is in water.
- **Floral Clay** is a waterproof adhesive that will adhere only to dry surfaces. It is used to attach a kenzan to a container. The clay comes in rolls as a flat tape, green or white, and remains flexible. A little goes a long way; stretch it thin as you apply.
- **Floral Foam** is a green brick that absorbs over 40 times its weight in water. (The holes in Instant *Oasis* accelerate absorption; Deluxe *Oasis*, which is denser than standard foam and over 30% stronger, is very useful for heavy stems, such as Gladiolus or tropicals.)

Stems may be inserted into wet foam at any angle, straight into the top or sideways, with the assurance that the flower will stay where you put it. To use, first saturate the foam by placing it, holes down, in a container filled with fresh water. Do not push the brick under water; just let it do its thing. When the water has reached the top of the brick, it is wet throughout.

Once the foam has been saturated, do not allow it to dry, as it will not reabsorb moisture. You can save wet foam by sealing it in plastic and storing it in the refrigerator. Wet foam is inert; if mold appears, it will have come from bacteria left by stems.

Carve floral foam to fit a container by making an impression of the container's opening on the foam (Fig. 22). Try not to compress the foam, as you push it into the container, and be sure to leave an opening at one side, so that you can feel the water level when you are replenishing.

Fig. 22

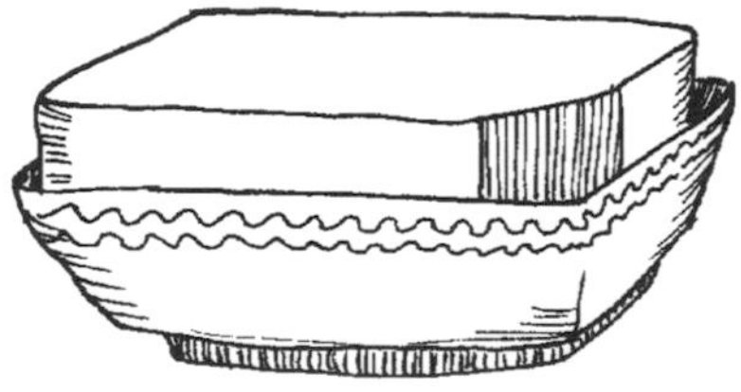

Fig. 22. Floral foam need not fill your container from side to side.

Rest the foam on the bottom of the container for stability, but let it protrude about 1" above the water level to allow for lateral placement of stems. Water will travel only about 1" into the foam above the water line, so place your stems accordingly.

Plan ahead; pulling stems in and out will crumble floral foam and destabilize your arrangement. Before inserting fleshy or soft stems, such as Tulips and Amaryllis, make a hole with a dowel. If you change your mind about the placement of a stem and decide to remove it, take the time to re-cut it before replacing it. Also, do not permit an air pocket to form by partially pulling a stem out of the foam. And, finally, avoid inserting a stem all the way through the foam, as it may lose contact with the water.

- **Glass Containers** require special mechanics. The stems attract attention, and any debris in the water creates a focal point. At a distance, an arrangement in glass may even appear to float. Here are some ideas:

Use glass marbles to stabilize your design; first, put the stems into the vase and then carefully drop the marbles in and around them.

Make a grid with clear waterproof tape over the top of a glass vase to hold your stems (Fig. 23).

Fig. 23

Fig. 23. Make sure you hide the tape with flowers or leaves.

Line your glass with crushed vinyl food wrap to camouflage the stems.

Products known as *Terra-sorb* and *Water Saver of New England* absorb hundreds of times their weight in water. Generally used for new plantings, they come as tiny dry crystals that swell when wet. In a tall glass bud vase, the crystals will look like bubbles and support a few stems.

- A **Hot-Glue Gun** provides a fast, easy way to place dried or silk materials on a styrofoam base or to attach moss around a container. Use it in the fall to make an everlasting wreath of Hydrangea. Because this glue dries immediately, you can also use it with shells or other heavy materials. Caution: Hot glue is very hot! Do not use with fresh flowers.
- A **Kenzan**, or pin-holder, is usually used in a shallow container to create a line design. Look for a kenzan that has needles at least 5/8" high to support your stems; it should be made of copper or have a heavy lead base that will not rust. Paint the pin-holder to blend with your container.

Use floral clay to attach a dry kenzan to the bottom of a dry container. Press the clay along the outer perimeter of the bottom of the kenzan, stretching the clay as you go (Fig. 24). Only a thin layer is necessary; a layer that is too thick will relax and cause the kenzan to tilt under the weight of your arrangement. Press the kenzan onto the bottom of the container using a twisting motion to form a suction between the bottom of the kenzan and the container.

Fig. 24

Fig. 24. Do not place a ball of floral clay in the center of your kenzan; apply a thin strip around the edge.

- **Plush-coated Wire** is used to make into "hair-pins" that will hold moss in place.
- **Turkey Wire** is like chicken wire but with a 2" grid. It is used in very large containers, instead of floral foam, to hold stems in water. Roses and Anemones, especially, are much happier in water than in foam. To use, cut a piece 2 times the size of the opening of your container. Roll this on the diagonal to fit, leaving 1"-2" extending above the top of the container for horizontal placement of stems. Using this mechanic takes practice. Although the larger holes in turkey wire allow sufficient space to insert stems, it soon becomes evident that it is very difficult to remove them. However, it is worth your effort to learn this method, because flowers last longest in water.

44

- **Urns** (cemetery) are green metal funnels that can be helpful when you are working with large arrangements. They hold water and are used to extend flowers higher in a design. A cemetery urn will hold floral foam and multiple blossoms.
- A **Water Pick**, a clear plastic tube that can be attached to a stake, is used to extend a flower's height (Fig. 25). They hold only one blossom. Unfortunately, even though they have covers, water must be added frequently, as a flower will drink a water pick dry over night.
- **Waterproof Tape**, which comes in green or clear, must be applied to a dry surface. Once attached, it will hold even if it gets wet. Place a cross of green tape over chicken wire that is covering floral foam and secure the tape to the sides of the dry container (Fig. 26). Use clear tape with glass containers.

Always cover your mechanics! Place stones over a pin-holder in a low dish, cover floral foam and wire with moss or foliage, and camouflage any part of a liner that will show by painting it moss green or brown. Securely placed and well camouflaged mechanics make any arrangement look more natural and more elegant.

Fig. 25

Fig. 25. Water picks are best used in designs that are to last only one day.

Fig. 26

Fig. 26. Hide the tape that comes over the sides of your container; if you use a liner, wrap the tape completely around it for stability.

45

Creating Arrangements

The best way to learn, of course, is by doing, so in this section we present several exercises in design that will produce lovely arrangements for your home. With each practice, you will develop the skills you need to create your own artistic designs.

One of the most important skills you will need is the ability to incorporate the following guidelines into all your floral creations. As you work through the exercises in this section, you will see how these general rules underlie each set of instructions.

First, choose a container and a design that will be in *proportion* to the space for which you are arranging. Using Fig. 27 as a reference, the length of your primary vertical line -- i.e., the height (C) of an arrangement above the rim -- should be 1 1/2 to 2 1/2 times the height (A) plus the diameter (B) of the container (Fig. 27).

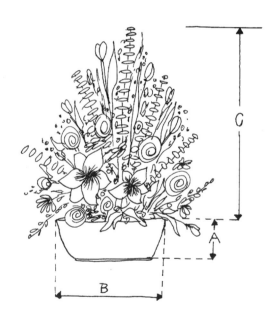

Fig. 27

Fig. 27. The determination of height within the range of 1 1/2 to 2 1/2 times (A + B) is an aesthetic decision that depends upon the materials and container you use.

Work out your mechanics before you begin arranging. If you are uncertain about some details — e.g., how to secure a pin holder with floral tape — you can refresh your memory by reviewing the preceding section on Mechanics. Next, fill your clean container with clean, fresh water to about the 3/4 mark; doing so will stabilize the container and assure that the conditioned flowers are never out of water.

Develop the habit of working on a lazy Susan. While essential for arrangements that will be viewed in the round, this method is always useful for checking symmetry, depth, *balance*, voids, etc.

Begin by establishing your line, which is the skeleton of your design. Complete placing all similar branches or flowers, before you proceed to another material. This order assures an even distribution of forms, textures, and colors throughout your design.

For example, if you are using Delphinium, Roses and Alstroemeria, place all the Delphinium first to establish your line. Next, place all your Roses, which are your *dominant* form. Last, place your Alstroemeria, a transitional form. When placing transitional material make sure that you stay within the established line.

Plant material should overlap but should not touch the edge of the container, nor should it touch the base (table top or floor), the background, or the wall. If properly conditioned, a stem will support its own flower or leaf.

Placing an accessory at the base of the container creates visual weight. The accessory can be a rock, a statue, a gourd, whatever you like. The object then becomes a part of the arrangement and should work with, not against, the rest of your design.

Following are illustrations to consider for various arrangements during different seasons.

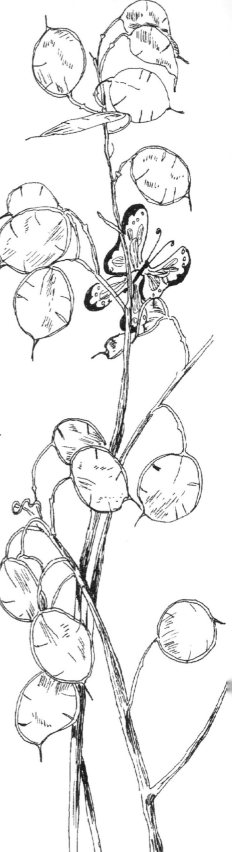

Designs for Spring

Spring #1

A line-mass design in an L pattern, to be viewed from all sides, for the living room coffee table (Fig. 28).

Materials:

- 6"-8" diameter saucer type container, deep enough to hold water to cover the pin-holder
- 2" pin-holder
- floral clay to attach pin holder to container
- pebbles
- lazy Susan
- 3 bare branches (Corkscrew Willow or Pussy Willow)
- 3 beardless Iris (2 flowers and 1 bud)
- 5 beardless Iris leaves

Add water to cover pin-holder; place container on lazy Susan.

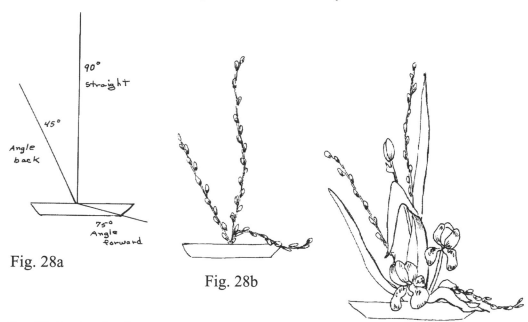

Fig. 28a

Fig. 28b

Fig. 28. Design for Spring #1.

Fig. 28c

Method:

1. Establish your line with Pussy Willow, placing the first stem into the center of the pin-holder. The height of this vertical line should be at least 1 1/2 times the height plus the diameter of your container; it must stand straight, not tipping forward or backward - *balance!*

The second Pussy Willow should be 2/3 the height of the first. Place it slightly behind and to the left of the first, slanting backward at a 45° angle but coming from the same area in the pin-holder (as a plant would grow).

The third Pussy Willow should be about 1/2 to 2/3 the height of the second. Place it in front of the first, slanting forward at a 75° angle and coming from the same area in the pin-holder. Do not cross stems.

2. Reinforce, do not alter, these lines with a second material, such as Iris leaves.

3. Add your Iris, placing the bud at the top of the design, the partially opened Iris low and below the center, and finally your *dominance*, the fully opened Iris, at or slightly above the rim.

Rotate your lazy Susan. The top points of all material should be at different heights and on different planes in this asymmetrical, open form. Cover the pin-holder with pebbles.

49

Spring #2

A **mass** design in a cone pattern, viewed from the front, for the hall table (Fig. 29).

Materials:

- 8" diameter x 4" high vegetable dish
- 1 block floral foam, soaked overnight and carved to fit container
- chicken wire to cover foam
- floral tape to secure foam and wire
- lazy Susan
- 9 branches, flowering purple Plum or Apple
- 18 Day Lily leaves
- 9 pink Peonies

Add water to 1" below top rim of container; place container on lazy Susan.

Method:

1. Establish your line with flowering branches. The tallest, thinnest branch, #1, should measure at least 1 1/2 times the height plus the diameter of the dish. [For this example, 1 1/2 x (8+4) = 18"] Place this branch just back of center in the container. This material must stand straight.

Cut four #2 size branches 3/4 the height of #1. Place one to the right and another to the left, slightly back of the first line; put the other two angling forward to the right and left coming out, as a plant would grow, from the base of #1.

Cut four #3 size branches 3/4 the height of #2. Place one to the right and another to the left and in front of #1, angling forward. Put another two branches to the right and left and in front of #1 angling forward but at a lower angle.

Rotate your lazy Susan. Look at your skeleton from the front. The tops of all branches should be at different heights, but symmetrical. Look at your skeleton from the right side and the left side. The tops of all branches should be on different planes.

2. Add Lily leaves to reinforce the lines of your branches.

3. Add Peonies, using a bud at the top and moving downward with increasing flower size. Be sure to place your largest flower centered at the base of the design, remembering to overlap the rim of the container.

Rotate your lazy Susan. Look for *balance and rhythm* within the design. Is it a conical pattern? Is it symmetrical?

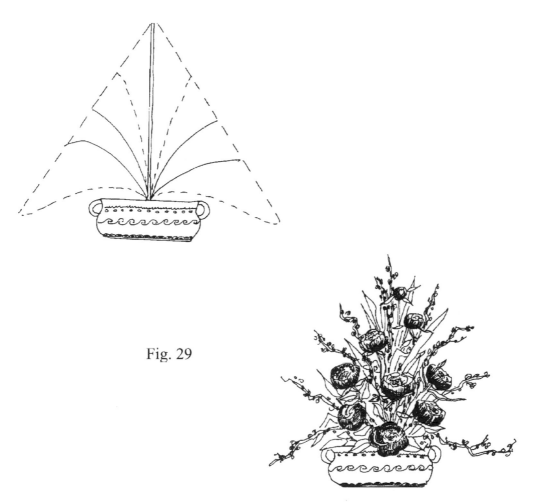

Fig. 29

Fig. 29. Design for Spring #2.

Designs for Summer

Summer #1

A **line** design for the dining table to be viewed from all sides (Fig. 30).

Materials:

- 8" diameter flat stone or shallow dish containing a 2" pin-holder
- 1 full bloom yellow Day Lily
- 3 Day Lily buds
- 6 Hosta leaves, yellow variegated

Add water to cover pin-holder; arrange on dining table.

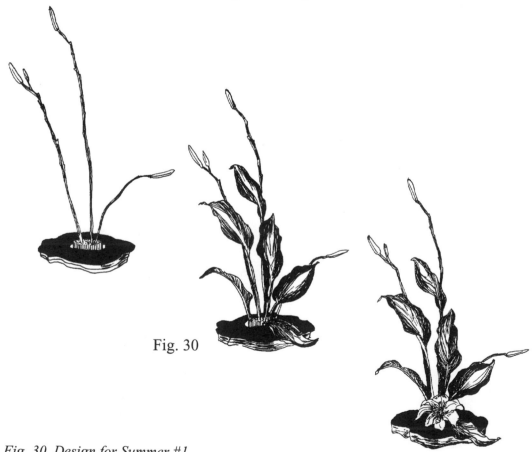

Fig. 30

Fig. 30. Design for Summer #1.

Method:

1. Establish your line with 3 Day Lily buds. Place the first stem in center of pin-holder. This stem should be about 12" high; it must stand straight. Place an 8" stem in the pin-holder at the same point and behind the first stem, angling back and left at a 15^0 angle. Place a 6" stem in the pin-holder at the same point as the first two, in front and angling forward at a 75^0 angle.

2. Place two Hosta leaves behind the first tallest bud. These leaves should be slightly shorter than the 12" stem they are reinforcing. Place two Hosta leaves in front of the 8" stem. Again, these leaves should be slightly shorter than the stem they are reinforcing. Place your two largest, but shortest, Hosta leaves to reinforce the 6" stem. Keep them low, so as to overlap the rim of the container, angling toward the center front.

3. Place the fully opened Lily low and centered. This is your *dominance*. The flower should overlap both the rim of the container and the lower Hosta leaf (Fig. 30).

Look at your arrangement from all sides. No two stems should be at the same height; you want depth and *balance.*

53

Summer #2

A mass design, white and green, in a sphere pattern, viewed from all sides, for the coffee table (Fig. 31).

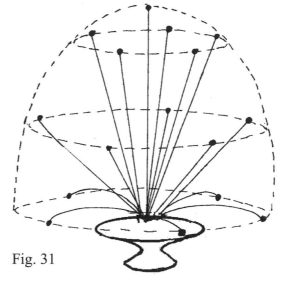

Fig. 31

Fig. 31. Design for Summer #2. Create a circle with 5 points. 4 points make a square.

Materials:
- 6" diameter x 4" high compote
- 1/2 block floral foam, soaked overnight and carved to fit container
- chicken wire to cover foam
- floral tape to secure wire and foam
- lazy Susan
- use green and white material from the garden or:

    16 stems Kerria japonica, variegated foliage

    20 leaves Iris, beardless

    16 stems Astilbe, white

    10 stems small spray Roses, white

    10 stems Bleeding Heart, white

Add water to 1" below top of container; place container on lazy Susan.

Method:

1. Establish your line for a sphere using the Kerria. Cut all 16 stems to a length that will extend above the rim at least 1 1/2 times the height plus the diameter of the container. [For this example, 1 1/2 x (6 + 4) = 15"]. Place the first vertical branch into the center of the foam. This line must stand straight.

Evenly distribute 5 branches around the perimeter of your container, inserting them into the foam at the point of the first branch and angling them outward (as a plant would grow). Do not allow the branches to rest on the rim of the container. Continue by placing 5 more branches higher up around the circle, staggering them among the first 5. Place your last 5 branches on a third plane around the circle, again evenly staggering them among the second 5. Looking at Fig.31, all branches must appear to come from the same point.

2. Reinforce the sphere with Iris leaves, but be careful to keep to your established lines. Rotate your lazy Susan to check all sides. Evenly distribute 5 bunches of Iris leaves, made up of 2 stems each, between the first and second circles of Kerria. Keep these leaves inside the outer circumference of the Kerria, so you achieve an in-and-out look. Add 5 more bunches of Iris leaves, made up of 2 stems each, between the second and third circles of Kerria keeping them inside, closer to that first center Kerria.

3. Distribute the Astilbe evenly among the Kerria, staying within your established pattern.

4. Evenly distribute the Bleeding Heart throughout the design.

5. Finally add the Roses. More *dominant* than Astilbe and Bleeding Heart, they should be placed last.

Rotate your lazy Susan. Is the arrangement still a sphere? Is it *balanced* and symmetrical? It is a closed form, but still the butterflies must pass through. (Note that even though the branches and stems for this arrangement come in even numbers, the instructions call for placing them mostly by groups of five thereby maintaining the interest generated by uneven numbers.)

Summer (late) #3

A small mass design in a spherical pattern for the dining table to be viewed from all sides (Fig. 32).

Materials:

- 4" x 4" round basket with liner (A glass jelly jar will add weight and stabilize a lightweight basket.)
- floral foam, soaked overnight, carved to fit liner and extending 1/2 " above rim. (You don't need chicken wire, because the lightweight stems in this design will not break up your foam.)
- lazy Susan
- 11 stems of Japanese painted Fern
- 15 stems of Coral Bell foliage
- 13 stems of Allium flowers (circle onion or chive flowers also have the small scale necessary for this design.)

Add water to 1" below top of rim; place container on lazy Susan.

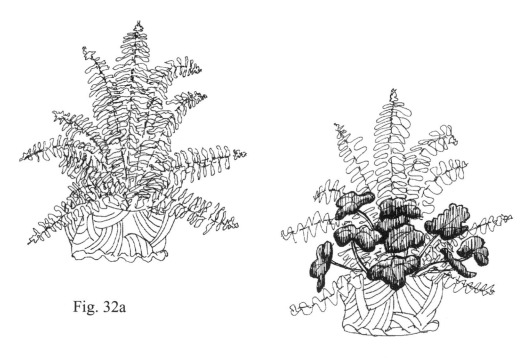

Fig. 32a

Fig 32b

Fig. 32c

Fig. 32. Design for Summer (late) #3.

Method:

1. Establish a spherical pattern with Japanese painted Fern. Cut 11 stems to a length that measures at least 1 1/2 times the height plus the diameter of your container (between 12" and 20"). Place the straightest stem in the center of the foam. Evenly distribute 6 Fern around the perimeter. Distribute the remaining 4 Fern evenly inside the outer circle of Fern.

2. Evenly distribute the 15 stems of Coral Bell foliage, placing some inside the pattern but being careful not to lose your established line.

3. Evenly distribute the Allium flowers throughout your pattern.

Rotate the lazy Susan. Is your pattern still symmetrical? Is all material *balanced* and does your design have depth?

Designs for Autumn

Autumn #1

A line-mass design in a horizontal cylindrical pattern for the mantel shelf (Fig. 33).

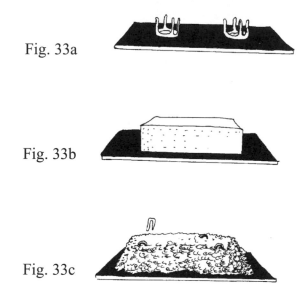

Fig. 33a

Fig. 33b

Fig. 33c

Materials:

- 6" x 4" tray to protect shelf from wet foam
- 1 block floral foam, soaked overnight and cut to 2" high x 5" long x 3" wide

  (Note: if the scale of these mechanics is inappropriate for your home, adjust the size of tray and foam to be in *proportion* to your mantel shelf.)
- 2 plastic anchor pins
- floral clay to secure anchor pins to tray
- sheet moss to cover foam on all sides except the bottom
- plush-coated wire to form 1" hairpins that will hold moss in place
- 8 stems Leucothoe
- 8 Viburnum trilobum branches with berries, also called Highbush Cranberry
- 10 stems of rose-colored Hydrangea

Carefully place moss-covered floral foam onto tray, pressing it down on anchor pins; place tray on mantel shelf.

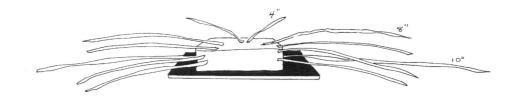

Fig. 33d

Fig. 33e

Fig. 33. Design for Autum #1.

Method:

1. Establish your line using Leucothoe. Cut 2 stems 10" long. Place these in the center of the right and left ends of the moss-covered brick, extending the horizontal line. Cut 4 stems 8" long. Place two stems toward the front of the brick, one at the right side and one at the left. Place 2 stems toward the back of the brick, one right and one left. Cut 2 stems 4" long; put these toward the center top of the brick, one extending right and one left. Keep your line low and horizontal.

2. Add Viburnum branches, distributing them evenly throughout your established line. These branches should be slightly shorter than the Leucothoe lines they are reinforcing. Allow some material to overlap the edge of the shelf.

3. Evenly distribute the Hydrangea throughout your design, keeping inside the pattern lines. Be sure to place the largest flower at the center for *dominance* and smaller flowers at the extremities.

Autumn #2

A small mass design in a spherical pattern for the dining table to be viewed from all sides (Fig. 34).

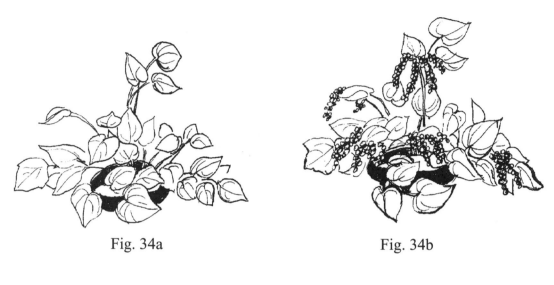

Fig. 34a   Fig. 34b

Fig. 34c

Fig. 34. Design for Autumn #2.

Materials:

- 3" x 4" bowl (A dull artichoke color works well with this material, or hollow out an artichoke for a container.)
- floral foam, soaked overnight and carved to fit container (Again, you will not need chicken wire to cover the foam.)
- lazy Susan
- 3 stems Epimedium
- 5 stems pink Roses, such as Betty Prior
- 7 stems Pieris japonica, andromeda, seed pods only

Add water to 1" below rim of container; place container on lazy Susan.

Method:

1. Establish your line with Epimedium. Prune the stems to make 6 pieces. The length of one piece should be at least 1 1/2 times the height plus the diameter of your container (between 11" and 17"). Place this stem in the center of the foam; be sure it stands straight. The remaining five stems should all measure approximately 3/4 the length of the first stem. Space these evenly around the perimeter of your container. Allow some leaves to overlap the rim.

2. With your fingers, gently ease open the small Roses to a full bloom. Distribute these 5 flowers evenly between the center Epimedium and the 5 Epimedium around the perimeter.

3. Remove the leaves from the Pieris japonica branches. (The pods are your third form and texture in this pattern.) Evenly distribute these stems within the design, placing some inside the sphere but being careful not to change the line.

Rotate the lazy Susan. Is your material balanced and symmetrical within the pattern? This is a closed form. Is there room for the butterfly?

Autumn #3

A small line design in an asymmetrical crescent for the hall table (Fig. 35).

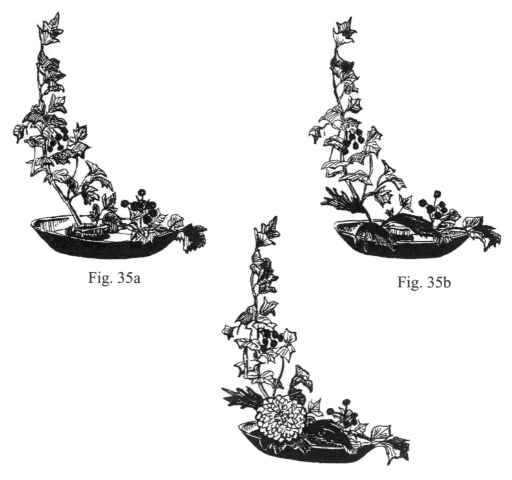

Fig. 35a

Fig. 35b

Fig. 35c

Fig. 35. Design for Autumn #3.

When you use a kensan, cut the stems flat for stability. If a stem is too thick to fit into the pins, cut it on a slant or taper the cut end. If a stem is too thin to hold its position in the pins, add a second piece of thicker stem. Insert the stem into the needles and gently bend it in the desired direction.

Materials:

- 6" long flat oval dish, deep enough to hold water to cover pin-holder
- 1" pin-holder
- floral clay to secure pin-holder
- sheet Moss
- 2 branches, e.g., Hickory or Viburnum (Look for curved branches.)
- 1 Dahlia
- 3 Peony leaves that have turned bronze

Add water to cover pin-holder; arrange on location.

Method:

1. Establish your line with the branch. Look for natural curving growth before cutting from a bush or tree. For this crescent design, you will need a top curved line 9" long and a bottom curved line 4" long. Possibly one branch, with pruning, will serve your needs.

Press the 9" branch into the center of the pin-holder, having it curve toward the right. If you are using a branch with leaves, look at the way it was growing; there will be a front or positive side and a back or negative side. Do not place it backwards. Press the 4" branch into the center of the pin-holder, so that it appears to be an extension of the upper line.

2. Place 1 Peony leaf angling backward from the center of your crescent. Place 2 Peony leaves angling forward, right and left, from the center of your crescent, allowing one to overlap the rim of your container.

3. Add 1 large Dahlia bloom at the center of the design. This is your *dominance*. (Three small Chrysanthemums in a cluster could substitute for the Dahlia.)

Cover pin-holder with sheet Moss. Do not allow the Moss to extend to outer rim of dish, as it will wick water onto the furniture.

Designs for Winter

Winter #1

A line-mass design in a symmetrical crescent pattern for the hall table (Fig. 36).

Fig. 36a

Fig. 36b

Materials:

- 1 candlestick about 10" high
- 1 O'DAPTER unit, foam soaked overnight
- 8 stems red-bark Dogwood, bare branch (Look for natural curves.)
- 6 stems Leucothoe
- 4 stems Umbrella Pine
- 16 stems red mini Carnations
- 1 red Anthurium

Arrange on location.

Method:

1. Establish your line with the red-bark Dogwood. Cut 2 curving branches 10" long; place them into foam, right and left, forming a crescent. Cut 2 curving branches 8" long; place them behind the first line, on a different plane but following the established crescent.

Cut 2 curving branches 6" long; put them in front of the first line, angling forward but following the established crescent. Cut 2 branches 4" long; angle these forward as well. All branches should come from the same point, as a plant would grow.

2. Cut 2 Leucothoe stems 10" long, 2 stems 8" long, and 2 stems 6" long. Reinforce the red-bark lines with these stems.

3. Cut 4 Umbrella Pine branches 5" long. Place these angling outward from the center of the foam.

4. Add the mini Carnations, carefully following the established crescent. Distribute these evenly among the greens.

5. Place the Anthurium in the center of the crescent, on the axis, slightly overlapping the rim of the candlestick. This is your *dominance.*

Look at your design. Does it have depth? Is it symmetrical?

This is a long-lasting arrangement. The red-bark Dogwood, Umbrella Pine, and Leucothoe will last for several months — so long as you add water to the floral foam — making it necessary to replace only the flowers.

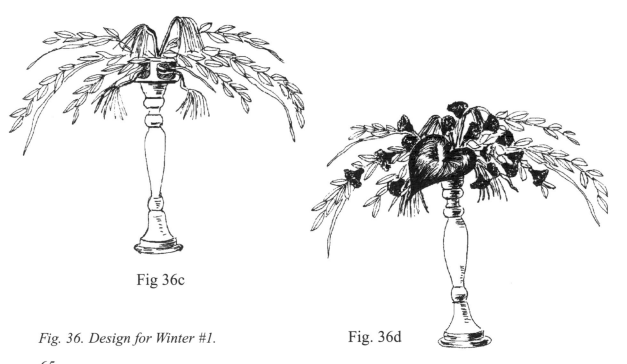

Fig 36c

Fig. 36. Design for Winter #1.

Fig. 36d

65

Winter #2

A line design in vertical pattern for the hall table (Fig. 37).

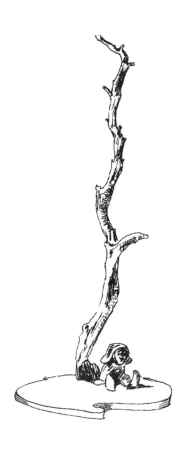

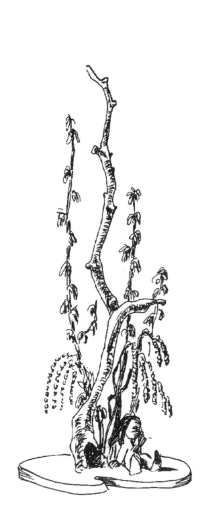

Fig. 37

Fig. 37. Design for Winter #2.

Materials:

- 1 branch (Look for a weathered branch with interesting lines).
- 5" x 5" piece of plywood
- 1" pin-holder in self-contained cup
- floral clay to secure pin-holder cup to plywood
- sheet moss
- 3 stems Hammamelis witch hazel
- 2 stems Pieris japonica andromeda
- 1 figure, an accessory of your choosing that works with the design

Attach the pin holder cup to the plywood and add water.

Method:

1. Screw the weathered branch to the plywood to establish your line.

2. In the pin holder, arrange three stems of blooming witch hazel of different lengths, one reaching almost to the top of the branch. Keep them close to the branch, so that you achieve a vertical line. (Forced Forsythia may be substituted for witch hazel.)

3. Place your figure in front of the branch.

4. Place two short stems of Pieris japonica low and close to the branch. They should overlap the pin-holder and the figure.

Cover pin-holder and plywood with dry sheet moss.

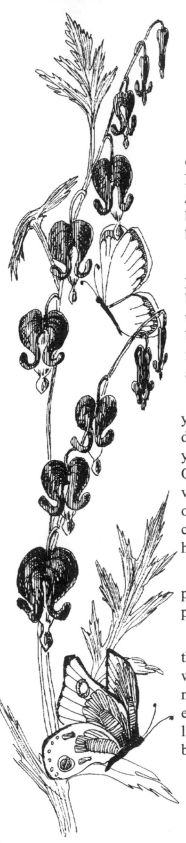

On Your Own in Any Season

First, identify the place in your home where you would most often like to see an arrangement. In the beginning, arrange only for this one location, and you will get to know it well. Next, plan your composition of flowers and container on a *scale* appropriate to the physical space you have chosen. It is to be hoped that you have already been collecting containers that blend in color and style with your home's interior.

A favorite bowl or dish may be your starting point, but if your garden happens to be filled with gorgeous flowers, then begin with the materials. Think about form, texture and color that will create lines with *balance* and *rhythm*. Practice combining flowers and containers — flowering branches in the family soup tureen, green foliage in a beanpot, or Narcissus in a wooden shoe.

Begin with only one color family. Within any single color, you will find a variety of form and texture with which to develop your sense of pattern. Using only white, for example, you can very successfully combine white Bleeding Heart, Queen Anne's Lace, and white Astilbe or Butterfly Bush with variegated Kerria. When you have mastered pattern with only one color, try several designs using tints and shades of one color family, such as pink, red and burgundy. Red, the primary hue, will be *dominant*. Place it near or at the axis.

Next, try complementary colors. Begin by using only one primary color and its complement — e.g., Lady's Mantle, purple Iris, and green foliage (Peony leaves or Umbrella Pine).

Establish your line, remembering pattern. For example, hold three Iris of different lengths loosely at the bottom, as they would grow. Let them take their spread, and you will have a natural design (Fig. 38). The stems in all your designs should emerge from a central point, as they would in nature. Once the line has been established, decide what your dominant color will be and then what material you will use to fill in your pattern.

68

When arranging for a large space or working in a very tall container, go higher. The height of the flowers above the rim must never be the same as the height of the container, measured from base to rim of opening, because repetition of two equal parts divides interest, producing double *dominance*. For the same reason, you would never place a tie-back in the middle of your drapery.

Every once in a while, you may want some new ideas. If the urge to experiment arises during the last week in April, come to Art in Bloom, where you will find more than a hundred exciting arrangements. Any other time of the year, come and browse in the galleries of the museum. Study floral still lifes, such as Jan van Huysum's *Vase of Flowers in a Niche* or Renoir's *Mixed Flowers in an Earthenware Pot*. What would you do differently? Notice the colors Thomas Sully uses in the portrait of his son, *The Torn Hat;* or Sargent's choice of colors in his portrait of *Mrs. Fiske Warren and Her Daughter*. You'll find inspiration in every room and on every wall.

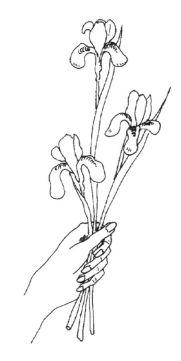

Fig. 38

Fig. 38. This simple experiment demonstrates how easy design can be.

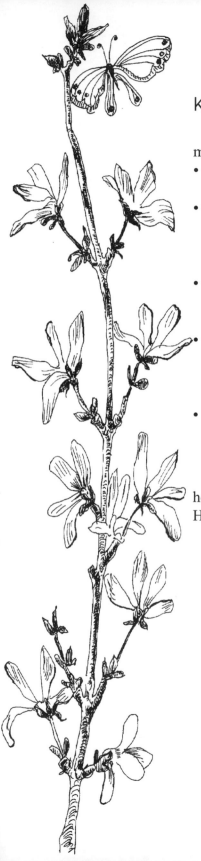

Keeping Your Material Alive

Once you have created an arrangement, you will enjoy it much longer, if you follow these simple procedures:

- Add clean water containing a floral preservative daily. The water level in a container can go down inches over night.
- Mist daily, if possible. (At Art in Bloom arrangers cannot mist, because the moisture that flowers love is very bad for works of art. There may be places in your home as well, where misting would do some harm.)
- Remember to leave a finger space in the mechanics, so you can check the water level. Use cool water; it is easier to feel.
- Remove spent flowers to encourage new blooms. Not only are they unsightly, but also they encourage a plant to make seed instead of opening new buds. Cut wilted flowers to remove; pulling them out might topple your entire design.
- To revive wilted flowers, re-cut the stems on a slant under water. Place stems into very hot water for one hour and then return to the arrangement.

Do not place fresh materials in a sunny window, on top of a heat source, under a lighting fixture or in front of a cold draft. Heat and drafts will cause them to wilt before their time.

Preserving Materials

Flowers and herbs dried during the growing season are especially appreciated in the middle of dreary winter months. An arrangement of dried flowers will survive virtually carefree, when heat has been turned on in the house and humidity is low. Herbs preserved fresh from the garden definitely retain better flavor and color than commercially packaged seasonings.

Harvesting for preservation is best done during the heat of the day when the plant is its driest; as you may recall, this is exactly the opposite of the time you would pick flowers to condition for fresh arrangements.

There are several ways to preserve plant material — air or oven drying, freezing and use of desiccating or saturating agents. With all these methods, however, trial and error still plays an important role, because plants vary so much from one to another and because conditions for preserving vary from home to home. In general, the more water contained in the material, the longer the required drying time. Also, during the drying process, material must be kept in a dark and dry location.

Most herbs dry easily, so let's begin with them.

Drying or Freezing Herbs

Green leafy herbs, such as Parsley, Basil, Tarragon and Chives, are very easy to work with. Watch them in your garden and remove any flowers as they appear. Herbs harvested just before flowering have the best flavor.

Snip Chives into short pieces. Remove stems from Parsley and similar forms and discard. Preserve only the leaves. At this point, either dry or freeze your herbs to preserve them.

To dry, spread cut herbs between layers of paper toweling, making sure they are not bunched, so they will not mold. Place in a basket and store where you have good air circulation, such as on top of the refrigerator. This method allows moisture to escape and keeps the herbs clean and the color good. Use a separate basket for each variety, as they dry at different rates.

You can also put herbs in a brown paper bag; tie the bag with a string, and hang it to dry. With this method, you must shake the bag daily to keep the leaves from molding.

71

To freeze, spread herbs on a cookie sheet, so that they do not stick together. When they are frozen, quickly place them in an air tight container for storage in the freezer.

Preserving Flowers and Leaves

As you gather floral material, keep in mind that blue, yellow, pink, and green retain their colors best. Reds and whites tend to turn brown, or even black.

Employing a desiccant for flowers and a saturant for foliage is the best way to preserve these materials for use in arrangements. Air and oven drying of flowers is still effective, but color and form will most likely alter.

With organic, non-toxic desiccants, good color is retained and the form of a flower can be almost perfect. Silica gel, used extensively in industry, is one of the fastest desiccants known. Although expensive, these products last for years and can be used over and over again by drying the crystals in an oven. With this method, only the flower heads are dried.

Cut each stem very short, 1/2" or less. Insert a short piece of light-weight wire (#26 or #28 guage) through the fleshy part of the upper stem and the flower head. When the flower has dried, usually in three to five days, the wire provides a stem with which to work.

Drying must be done in air tight containers, such as metal cookie tins. Place a 1/4" layer of silica gel in the bottom of the container. Gently place the fresh flower heads on top and carefully cover with more silica gel. You can layer flat shapes, such as Queen Anne's Lace, as long as the flowers are separated by gel. The more slowly and gently the crystals are applied, the better the shape and condition of the dried bloom.

Tape the tin tight to keep dampness out. Timing varies with the type of flower and the amount of moisture within each one. You should peek during the process; if your flowers dry too much, they will crumble and fall apart. When you think they are dry, carefully pour off the crystals. Then, to complete the procedure, put the flowers back on top of the crystals for one week, again taping the top of the tin.

After one week, pack the flowers carefully and loosely in a new tin, adding one tablespoon of fresh silica gel to the bottom, and tape the container closed. Mark the contents and store the preserved material until mid-November or until indoor humidity is diminished. When you open your tins again, you'll have wonderful materials for a dried arrangement.

You can also air dry bouquets, as was done in colonial times. This system works well for most field flowers, some garden flowers, and most herbs.

First, remove all foliage from flower stems; then, bind the stems loosely together and hang upside down in a warm, dark, and dry area. For binding, a rubber band is better than string, because stems shrink as they dry and the elastic contracts with them. If string is used, the stems will fall as they dry.

It is important to keep flowers and leaves in the dark to preserve color. If you do not have an attic or barn to dry in, place a brown paper bag over your material, tie it closed, and hang it in the kitchen. Moisture will pass through the paper during the drying process, and the bag will keep the material dark and clean. Do not use plastic as the petals will mold.

Microwave drying, although successful, is very much a trial and error method, because each flower behaves differently. Follow the directions printed in your Microwave Cook Book.

The best way to preserve foliage is to saturate it in a glycerin solution of one part glycerin to three parts hot water. Before inserting it into the solution, crush or cross-cut the cut end of a branch of leaves, such as Beech. Keep the stem in the solution until moisture begins to drip off the topmost leaf, indicating that the entire branch is saturated.

At that point, you can remove the branch from the glycerin solution and store it without water. It should keep for at least one year, and it will be a welcome source of material for your designs.

73

Creating Dried Arrangements

Organize your mechanics first, using the dry floral foam manufactured for this purpose. (See Appendix B, Supplies.)

Next, lengthen the wire or air-dried stems of your flowers by adding wire with green floral tape. Insert these wire stems carefully into the foam, working from the center of the design outward because this material is very fragile. Then, spray your completed arrangement with a fixative to prevent the materials from absorbing moisture from the air.

Dried designs are best used as table centerpieces or in locations where they are somewhat protected — not in direct sunlight, which will fade color. As with fresh arrangements, use your imagination. Express your own personality, and have fun.

Potpourri

When a fresh arrangement is beginning to look tired, you can transform the flowers into potpourri, a colorful mixture of dried petals and scented oils. Use the same method as you used to dry herbs. (See above.)

Your greatest problem is mildew and mold. So, begin by removing the petals from the flowers to release moisture as quickly as possible. Dry the petals in a dark and dry location, remembering that air circulation is critical. Only when the petals are completely dry are they ready to be stored or used in potpourri.

Store in an opaque ceramic or glass container with a cover, such as an old pickle crock. Even though the petals are dry, prolonged exposure to light will destroy their color. Do not use plastic, as it can be porous and allow moisture inside. Do not use metal, as it interferes with scent.

To make your potpourri, add oils and fixative. Mix and leave to blend for at least one month. The wonderful perfume of potpourri comes from these added oils. Dried petals are only the vehicle, because they have very little scent after drying. Many concentrated oils are available, and your choice of scents depends on personal preference. Below are two recipes to get you started.

Although fixatives, such as Orris Root or Calamus, will delay the loss of scent, in time the fragrance will dissipate. When it does, simply add more oils. As you can see, collecting and drying flower petals is the biggest labor in making potpourri.

Potpourri Recipes

Rose Scent
- 3 gallons dry petals, use pink and blue
- 8 ounce dried French Lavender flowers
- 4 ounce Calamus
- 1/2 ounce Muguet (Lily-of-the-valley) oil
- 1/2 ounce Rose Geranium oil
- 3/4 ounce. Rose oil
- 1/2 ounce Lavender oil

Lemon Scent
- 3 gallons dry petals, use yellow and green
- 1 quart Mint leaves
- 4 ounce Calamus
- 3/4 ounce Lemon oil
- 1/2 ounce Verbena oil
- 1/4 ounce Bergamot oil

NOTES

Appendix A

Garden Plants for the Flower Arranger to Grow

The following list of perennials, shrubs and trees are easily grown in the garden and provide a basis for floral arrangements throughout the year.

ACHILLEA filipendulina 'Gold Plate' Yarrow: Flowers are long lasting and dry well.

ALCHEMILLA Ladies mantle: Use flowers and foliage. Self seeding and hardy.

ALLIUM Chives, onion: Arrange flowers, eat leaves in salad.

AQUILEGIA Garden columbine: Both flowers and foliage are useful.

ARBORVITAE: Evergreen, plant in full sun.

ARTEMESIA absinthium: Silver foliage, grows to 4 feet; used to make autumn wreaths when dried.

ARTEMESIA 'Silver King': Silver foliage for arranging.

ASARUM europeaum European ginger: Plant in shade. Use in bud vases.

ASTILBE: White, pink or red flowers, tolerates shade. Use in summer arrangements.

ATHYRIUM niponicum Japanese painted fern: Use with feverfew and Fairy rose. Hardy and spreading but not invasive.

CORNUS stolonifera Redtwig and yellowtwig dogwood: Use bare branches in the winter.

CORNUS kousa Kousa dogwood: Flowers last long into the summer. Disease resistant.

CORYLUS avellana 'Contorta' Harry Lauder's walking stick: Use for line material without foliage.

COTINUS coggygria 'Royal Purple' Purple smokebush: Good burgundy line material.

COTONEASTER divaricata: Plant in sun or shade. Strong foliage and fast growing.

DEUTZIA gracilus: White flowers force well in the springtime; also good line material.

DICENTRA spectabilis Bleeding heart: Summer foliage is as valuable as the springtime flowers.

77

EPIMEDIUM pinnatum sp. colchicum: Valuable foliage lasting long into the winter.

EUONYMUS fortunei 'Silver Queen': Long lasting variegated foliage.

EUONYMUS alatus Burning bush,wing-bark: Valuble line material with or without foliage.

FICUS lyrata Fiddle-leaf fig: House plant; dramatic foliage all year.

FORSYTHIA: Forces well in the springtime; good line material.

HAMAMELIS x intermedia Witch hazel: Flowers in January or February.

HEDERA helix Ivy: Evergreen and long lasting when cut. Can be invasive.

HELIANTHUS tuberosus Jerusalem artichoke: Good summer flowers.

HEMEROCALLIS Daylily: Both foliage and flowers are very useful.

HEUCHERA Coral bells: Both flowers and foliage are useful.

HOSTA, all species: Valuable foliage available in yellow-greens, blue-greens and variegated.

HYDRANGEA paniculata: Blooms on current season's growth. Drys well. Prune severly in the winter to control plant size.

ILEX verticillata Winterberry: Red berries last through the winter. Plant male and female.

IRIS, Beardless species: Use foliage all summer.

KERRIA japonica 'Variegata': Good line material.

LEUCOTHOE: Evergreen, plant in shade. Extremly long lasting when cut.

MALUS Apple, crabapple: Forces in early spring; good summer foliage.

PACHYSANDRA: Evergreen, valuable for covering mechanics.

PELARGONIUM, Scented-leaved geranium: House plant, long lasting, edible and fragrant.

PAEONIA Peony: Use foliage all summer.

PIERIS japonica Lily-of-the-vally bush, andromeda: Broad leaf evergreen,
 flowers early in the spring.

POLYGONATUM biflorum Solomon's seal: Good line material.

PRUNUS japonica 'Thundercloud' Flowering plum: Good burgundy foliage.

ROSA 'Betty Prior': Continuous bloom throughout the season. Disease resistant.

ROSA 'Fairy': Almost continuous bloom throughout the season. Disease resistant.

RUDBECKIA Brown-eyed Susan: Tolerates hot, dry conditions.

SALIX discolor Pussy willow: Early spring line material.

SALIX matsudana'Tortuosa' Corkscrew willow: Good line material. Use as a bare branch.

SCIADOPITYS verticillata Japanese umbrella Pine: Evergreen. Very long lasting when cut.

STACHYS olympica Lambs' ears: Silver foliage.

TANACETUM parthenium Feverfew: Sometimes blooms twice during growing the season. Use foliage all summer. Self seeding for next years growth.

Appendix B
Supplies

When I first became interested in working with flowers, I realized I needed a collection of tools that would be used only for flower arranging. I started with a flat berry basket to hold my clippers, some pin-holders, a block of floral foam and a few water picks. Soon my collection grew, as I know yours will. I've found that the well equipped arranger will have the following:

Alcohol: Isopropyl (rubbing) type used to clean flower clippers after each daily use.

Alcohol: Grain variety used as an additive to certain conditioning waters.

Anchor pins: Small, round plastic disks with four prongs to secure floral foam in a dry shallow container, attached with floral clay.

Baster: Meat baster useful for filling bud vases or siphoning water off over filled containers.

Buckets: Deep, plastic buckets to hold water for conditioning.

Cemetery urns: Conical metal or plastic waterproof funnels used to elevate flowers in a very large design.

Chlorine bleach: Household type for cleaning conditioning buckets.

Clippers: Sharp, double-bladed or scissor-type used specifically to cut flower stems. Never cut wire with stem clippers!

Concentrated oils: Additives for the perfume in potpourri.

Drop cloth: Spread on the floor when arranging to catch trash.

Dry floral foam: Brown foam bricks that do not absorb water. Used for arranging dry or silk flowers.

Elastics: 4"-6" circumference for attaching materials to finished furniture or to hold moss in place when decorating containers.

Fixative spray: Used to seal in moisture on tropicals and delicate blooms.

Floral adhesive tape: Available in green and clear rolls; waterproof after attaching to a dry surface; unique qualities differ from cellophane tape or corsage tape.

Floral clay: Available in green or white rolls. Used to attach pin holders or any mechanic to a dry container. Can be removed with paint thinner. Not recommended for silver.

Floral corsage tape: A waxed stretchy tape used to cover wire and stems. Available in brown, green and white.

Floral foam: Green bricks that absorb over 40 times their weight in water. Used as a staple mechanic.

Floral glue: For fresh material.

Glue: Hot glue gun for dried and silk material.

Glycerin: Used to preserve leaves. Make a solution of one part glycerin to three parts hot water.

Kenzans (pin-holders): Heavy copper disk with 5/8" needles used to support stems in a shallow container

Knife: Used to sculpture floral foam, 10" blade, preferably.

Lazy Susan: Arranging on a lazy Susan reminds you to put depth into your design.

Liners: Waterproof containers of various sizes to use inside non-water-proof containers or inside silver containers.

Lopping shears: Heavy duty pruners for thick branches.

Moss: Grey, airy Spanish moss used to cover mechanics or enhance tropicals; green sheet moss used to cover mechanics and to enhance containers.

Paint: Spray can of moss green used to camouflage wire and liners.

Pebbles: Small and clean to add stability to lightweight containers, bud vases, or baskets.

Plastic bags: Used to cover cut, conditioned stems during transport.

Pliers: To cut wire and tighten wire.

Raffia: Used to secure moss on containers and to tie bouquets.

Rose stripper: Tongs with notches used to strip leaves and thorns from stems; plastic preferred.

Ruler: For measuring containers and areas in design space.

Scissors: To cut string and elastics from bundled flowers, but not for stems!

Silica gel: Used to preserve/dry fresh flowers.

Stakes: Thin green garden type for adding height to water picks and for supporting weak or hollow stems, such as Amaryllis.

String: Green florist's string used as a mechanic to tie wandering blossoms or to hold moss onto a perpendicular surface without being seen.

Stones: Decorative small rocks to cover mechanics, especially those used with a kenzan.

Styrofoam: Various shapes for working with fruits, vegetables, silk and dry materials.

Tape measure: To measure areas, such as tables, and to lay out dimensions of the design.

Tin snips: Special heavy duty scissors for cutting chicken and turkey wire.

Towels: To wipe up water spills and to dry containers before placing on finished furniture.

Turntable (lazy Susan): Necessary for all design projects.

Water picks: Small plastic tubes with removable covers; made to hold one stem; for adding height to a flower in large designs.

Watering can: To add water to arrangements daily.

Wire cutters: Plier-type made for cutting wire. Never use for flowers.

Fig. 40

Wire: Spools of 26 and 30 gauge green wire for aid with mechanics. Fig. 40

Chicken wire: (1" openings) used to cover floral foam for added stability or to sculpture into shapes to be used as containers.

Plush-coated wire: Lengths used to make "hair pins" for securing sheet moss; may also be used to strengthen hollow stems.

Turkey wire: (2" openings) used as a mechanic inside a large container for arranging in water.

APPENDIX C
Alphabetical Flower List for Conditioning

The following list is in addition to the section on Conditioning. All flowers require floral preservatives added to their water as described in the chapter on conditioning and some flowers require special treatment during this hydrating process. The vase life of a flower is also dependent on the time lapse between harvest and receiving it for conditioning. When you are planning to use a flower for a special occasion, experiment in advance to know how it will perform. My phrase "long lasting" refers to the vase life of the material as used in an arrangement after conditioning.

ACACIA Mimosa: Crush or cross-cut stems and condition in hot vinegar water. Does not last long.

ACER palmatum Japanese maple: Submerge entire branch in cool water for two hours. Crush or cross-cut stems, peel bark 1"-2" and condition in hot water. Does not last long, difficult to condition. Forces successfully.

ACHILLEA Yarrow: Cut stems under water and condition in warm water. Contact with foliage or bulb may cause skin irritation.

ACONITUM Monkshood: Cut stems under water and condition in warm water. All parts toxic. Foliage may irritate skin.

AGAPANTHUS Lily of the Nile: Cut stems under water, remove bottom white portion of stem and condition in cool water.

AGLAONEMA 'Silver King' Chinese evergreen: Cut stems under water and condition in cool water one hour or less. Long lasting.

ALBIZIA related to Acacia, a tropical shrub: Crush or cross-cut stems, peel bark 1"-2" and condition in warm water.

ALCHEMILLA Lady's mantle: Cut stems under water and condition in cool water. Long lasting. Can be air dried.

ALLIUM Chives, Onion: Cut stems under water, condition in cool chlorine water; any warmth increases onion odor, chlorine helps control strong odor. Preserve seed head by air drying. Contact with foliage or bulb may cause skin irritation.

ALMOND: see Prunus.

ALOE: Can be used without water.

ALPINIA purpuata, TAPEINOCHILUS ananassae Red ginger, tropicals: Do not refrigerate, keep in warm (45-50 degrees F.) and humid area. Cut stems under water and condition in warm water with preservative added. Spray with fixative before arranging. Avoid drafts and heat sources. Long lasting, many species lasting more than two weeks.

ALSTROEMERIA Peruvian lily: Cut stems under water and condition in cool water. Long lasting. Contact with flower or foliage may cause skin irritation.

AMARANTHUS cruentus Purple amaranth: Pick in full color. Boil stem ends and condition in cool vinegar water. Air dry, preserves well, holds color.

Amaryllis: see HIPPEASTRUM.

ANANAS bracteatus Wild pineapple, miniature pink and green fruits on a stem: Condition in hot water. Long lasting as are most menbers of the Bromeliad family. Can be dried by hanging.

Andromeda: see PIERIS floribunda, PIERIS japonica.

ANEMONE coronaria Windflower, poppy anemone: Boil stem ends and condition in cool water. Arrange in water, avoid floral foam. Does not last long. Sap may irritate skin.

ANETHUM graveolens Dill: Pick when in full color. Submerge entire stem in cool water for one hour, remove, cut stems under water and condition in warm water. Can be air dried.

ANIGOZANTHOS Kangaroo-paw: Cut stems under water and condition in warm water. Long lasting.

ANTHRISCUS sylvetris Queen Anne's lace: Submerge flower heads for one hour in cool water. Cut stems under water and condition in deep cool water. Long lasting.

ANTHURIUM andraeanum: Do not refrigerate, keep in a warm (55-60 degrees F.) and humid area. Cut stems under water and condition in warm water containing a preservative. Use fixative because so much moisture is lost through the flower head. Avoid drafts and extremes in temperature. Wilting flowers can be submerged in room temperature water for fifteen minutes. Very long lasting, 14-28 days. Will hold 24 hours out of water. Sap may irritate skin. All parts cause severe discomfort if ingested.

ANTIRRHINUM Snapdragon: Cut stems under water (if greenhouse forced, boil stem) and condition in cool water. Flower spikes bend toward a light source. Long lasting.

Apple: see MALUS.

AQUILEGIA Garden columbine: Cut stems under water, avoid wetting flower, and condition in warm water.

ARTEMISIA absinthium Wormwood: Pick in August before flowers appear. Boil stems and condition in hot water. Long lasting. Hang to dry.

ARTEMISIA 'Silver King' Sagebrush: Cut stems under water and condition in warm water.

ASARUM europaeum European ginger: Submerge leaves in cool water two hours. Remove, cut stems under water and condition in cool water.

ASPARAGUS densiflorus 'Sprengeri' Asparagus fern: Submerge in room temperature water for two hours. Remove, cut stems under water and condition in warm water.

ASPARAGUS densiflorus cv. Ming fern: Submerge in water for one hour. Remove, cut stems under water and condition in warm water.

ASPIDISTRA elatior Cast-iron plant: Condition in cool water. Long lasting.

ASTER garden annual: Cut stems under water, split stems and condition in hot sugar water. Hydrate in a separate bucket, tends to foul conditioning water. Does not last long.

ASTER cv. Michaelmas daisy, aster: Cut stems under water and condition in cool water. Hydrate in a separate bucket, tends to foul conditioning water. Longer lasting than garden asters.

ASTER pringlei 'Monte Cassino' September weed: Remove leaves that will be below water. Cut stems under water and condition in warm water. Long lasting.

ASTILBE: Cut stems under water and condition in warm water. Does not last long.

Azalea: see RHODODENDRON.

Baby's Breath: see GYPSOPHILA.

Bachelor's buttons, Cornflower: see CENTAUREA cyanus.

BAMBUSA Bamboo: Place stem ends in boiling vinegar water for three minutes. Condition in hot alcohol water. Does not last long.

Banana - see MUSA cv.

BANKSIA: Remove only the foliage that will be under water. Cut stems under water and condition in warm water with preservative added. Keep in a humid, 45-50 degrees F. area away from heat and drafts. Add water with preservatives frequently and recut stems when possible. Do not treat these flowers like succulents.

Basil: see OCIMUM basilicum.

Beech: see FAGUS.

BEGONIA: Flowers - boil stems and condition in cool water. Arrange in water. Branches - submerge entire branch in cool water for two hours. Remove, boil stem ends and condition stems in cool water. Arrange in water.

Bellflower: see CAMPANULA.

Bells of Ireland: see MOLUCCELLA laevis.

BETULA Birch: Crush or cross-cut stems, peel bark 1" - 2" and condition in hot water. Long lasting.

Birch: see BETULA.

Bird-of-Paradise: see STRELITZIA reginae.

Bittersweet: see CELASTRUS scandens.

Bleeding Heart: see DICENTRA spectabilis.

Blueberry, high-bush: see VACCINIUM corymbosum.

BOUVARDIA: Cut stems under water and condition in warm water.

Bridal Wreath: see SPIRAEA prunifolia.

Brown-eyed Susan: see RUDBECKIA.

BROMELIAD: Do not refrigerate. Condition in warm water. This is an air plant; long lasting out of water. Leaves tolerate stapling and gluing.

BUDDLEIA davidii Butterfly bush: Crush or cross-cut stem ends and condition in hot water. Does not last long.

Bugbane: see CIMICIFUGA.

Butterfly bush: see BUDDLEIA davidii.

CALADIUM: Place cut stems in boiling water for 15 seconds. Remove and submerge entire leaf in cool water for two hours. Condition in warm water. Wire leaf for support. Does not last long. Foliage and sap may irritate skin. All parts cause severe discomfort if ingested.

Calla Lily: see ZANTEDESCHIA.

CALLUNA Heather: Crush or cross-cut stems and condition in hot water. Does not last long. Air dry.

CAMELLIA: Submerge entire stem with flowers in cool water for two hours. Remove, split stems and condition in hot water. Wire flower to stem for support. Flower does not absorb water through stem, mist or spray flowers with fixative.

CAMPANULA Bellflower: Cut stems under water and condition in cool water. Does not last long.

Candytuft, perennial: see IBERIS sempervirens.

Carnation: see DIANTHUS.

CARTHEMUS tinctorius Safflower: Cut stems under water and condition in hot water. Long lasting.

Cattail: see TYPHA.

CELASTRUS scandens American bittersweet: Cut when berries are still green; orange berries will open over night when brought inside. Best to use dry. Remove leaves and spray with fixative or clear acrylic. Invasive, do not plant.

CELOSIA Cockscomb: Place stems in boiling water 15 seconds. Remove and condition in warm water. Air dry.

CENTAUREA cyanus Bachelor's button, cornflower: Cut stems under water and condition in cool water. Does not last long. Air drys well by hanging up-side-down, holds color.

CERCIS canadensis Eastern redbud: Crush or cross-cut stems, peel bark 1"-2" and condition in hot water. Long lasting. Forces successfully.

CHAENOMELES japonica Japanese flowering quince: Crush or cross cut stems, peel bark 1"-2" and condition in hot water. Forces sucessfully. Does not last long.

Cherry: see PRUNUS.

Chinese Evergreen: see AGLAONEMA 'Silver King'.

Chives: see ALLIUM.

CHRYSANTHEMUM: Pick in full bloom. Split stems and condition in warm sugar water in a separate bucket. Long lasting.

CHRYSANTHEMUM leucanthemum Marguerite: Pick in full bloom. Split stems and condition in warm water in a separate bucket. Long lasting.

CIMICIFUGA Bugbane: Cut stems under water and condition in cool water.

CITRUS limon Lemon leaf: Crush or cross-cut stems and condition woody stems in hot water. Long lasting.

CLEMATIS: Submerge flowers in cool water one hour. Remove, cut stems under water and condition in warm alcohol water. Dry in silica gel.

CLEOME Spider flower: Remove seed spines. Cut stems under water and condition in cool water. Does not last long.

COCCULUS: Condition stems in hot water. Long lasting.

Cockscomb: see CELOSIA.

Coffee foliage: see POLYSCIAS quilfoylei.

Columbine garden: see AQUILEGIA vulgaris cv.

CONSOLIDA Larkspur: Cut stems under water and condition in warm water. Spray with fixative for longer vase life. Can be dried in a desiccant.

CONVALLARIA Lily-of-the-valley: Submerge in cool water for 1/2 hour, remove bottom white portion of stem. Cut stems under water and condition in cool water. After conditioning, they will hold out of water for six hours. Use in clusters when arranging. Poisonous if ingested.

Coral Bells: see HEUCHERA.

Cornflower: see CENTAUREA cyanus.

CORNUS Dogwood: Crush or cross-cut stems, peel bark 1" - 2" and condition in hot water. Forces well but flowers tend to be small and dull in color. Do not force branches longer than two feet. Dry individual flowers in silica gel.

CORNUS stolonifera Redtwig dogwood and yellowtwig dogwood: Use as a bare branch in the winter. Leaves do not hold well.

CORYLINE terminalis Ti tree: Do not refrigerate, this is tropical foliage. Cut stems under water and condition in room temperature water with preservative added. Cover bucket with plastic to keep humidity high. Long lasting 7-14 days.

COSMOS bipinnatus Cosmos: Cut stems under water and condition in cool sugar water. Short lived.

COTINUS coggygria 'Royal Purple' Purple smokebush: Crush or cross-cut stems and condition in hot water. Long lasting.

COTONEASTER: Crush or cross-cut stems and condition in hot water. Long lasting.

CRABAPPLE: see MALUS.

CROCOSMIA: see TRITONIA.

CYCAS Sago palm: Do not refrigerate, this is tropical foliage. Cut stems under water and condition in room temperature water. Long lasting, 3-6 weeks. Can be used in a design out of water.

CYPERUS papyrus Papyrus: Cut stems under water, arrange in water. Does not last long.

Daffodil: see NARCISSUS

DAHLIA: Pick in bud. Boil cut stems and condition in warm, sugar water. Does not last long.

Daisy Native wild flower: Cut stems under water and condition in cool, sugar water. Dry in silica gel.

Daylily: see HEMEROCALLIS.

DELPHINIUM: Cut when first floret opens. Turn upside down to fill hollow stem with cool water and plug with cotton or floral foam. Carefully right flower stem and condition in warm water. Does not last long. Dry in silica gel. Foliage may irritate skin. All parts cause severe discomfort if ingested.

DEUTZIA gracilis: Submerge entire branch in cool water for one hour. Remove, crush or cross-cut stems, peel bark 1"-2" and condition in hot water. Forces well.

DIANTHUS Carnation: Cut stems under water between joints, do not break stem at joints, water does not absorb through the blunt joint. Condition in cool water. Long lasting.

DICENTRA spectabilis Bleeding heart: Split stems and condition in cool salted water. Forces successfully. Leaves are long lasting. Dry in silica gel.

DIGITALIS Foxglove: Cut stems under water, condition in warm alcohol water. All parts are toxic and may cause skin irritation.

Dill: see ANETHUM graveolens.

Dock: see RUMEX.

Dogwood: see CORNUS.

Dogwood, redtwig and yellowtwig: see CORNUS.

DRACAENA fragrans: Do not refrigerate, this is tropical foliage. Submerge entire leaf in body temperature water for one hour. Remove, cut stems under water and condition in room temperature water. Cover bucket with plastic for humidity. Very long lasting, 8 weeks or more.

ECHINOPS Globe thistle: Boil cut stems and condition in warm water. Long lasting. Air dries successfully.

ENKIANTHUS: Crush or cross-cut stems, peel bark 1" - 2" and condition in hot water. Forces well.

EPIMEDIUM pinnatum sp. colchicum: Cut stems under water and condition in cool water.

EREMURUS Foxtail lily: Cut stems under water and condition in cool water. Long lasting.

ETLINGERA elatior Torch ginger: Do not refrigerate, keep in warm (45-50 degrees F.) and humid area. Cut stems under water and condition in warm water. Keep vertical or flowers will take a bend. Spray with fixative before arranging. Lasts less than one week.

EUCALYPTUS: Crush or cross-cut stems and condition in hot water. Air dry. Penetrating odor. Long lasting.

EUONYMUS: Crush or cross-cut stems and condition in hot water. Long lasting. To keep, seal in plastic bags and keep in a cool, dark area. All parts cause severe discomfort if ingested.

EUPATORIUM purpureum Joe Pye weed: Pick when color first shows. Submerge entire flower and stem for one hour. Remove and condition in cool water. Can be air dried.

EUPHORBIA pulcherrima Poinsettia: Cut stems under water. Boil or burn stems to stop flow of milky substance, do not remove leaves. Condition in warm water. Does not last long. All parts toxic. Sap may irritate skin.

EUSTOMA grandiflorum Lisianthius: Cut stems under water and condition in cool water. Long lasting.

Evergreens, needled: Crush or cross-cut stems and condition in hot water. When cut in the fall, after a deep freeze, sprinkle with water and seal in a plastic bag. Keep in a cool, dark area. Most needled evergreens will hold from October through December. When arranging use a fixative spray. Do not use Hemlock indoors, it dries out quickly. All parts of yew are toxic, Taxus Baccata.

FAGUS Beech: Submerge entire branch in cool water for two hours. Remove, crush or cross-cut stems, peel bark 1" - 2" and condition in hot water. May be preserved in a glycerin solution.

Ferns: Submerge in cool water one hour. Remove and condition stems in warm water. Ferns are difficult, test before using. Japanese painted fern and Christmas fern from the garden are usually successful.

Feverfew: see TANACETUM parthenium.

FICUS lyrata Fiddle-leaf fig: Boil or burn stems, to stop flow of milky substance, and condition in warm water. Long lasting.

Fiddle-leaf fig: see FICUS lyrata.

FORSYTHIA: Crush or cross-cut stems, peel bark 1" - 2" and condition in hot water. Long lasting. Forces successfully.

Foxglove: see DIGITALIS.

Foxtail lily: see EREMURUS.

FREESIA: Cut stems under water and condition in cool water. Long lasting.

FUCHIA: Boil or burn stems and condition in warm water. Does not last long. Dry in silica gel. Best used as a potted plant.

Funkia: see HOSTA.

GALAX: Submerge leaves in cool water for one hour. Remove and seal in a plastic bag. Keep in cool, dark area. Long lasting even out of water. Can be stapled or glued.

GARDENIA: Submerge flower in cool water 1/2 hour. Remove, cut stem under water and condition in warm water. Mist flowers and leaves. Will hold out of water, after conditioning, for six hours.

GENISTA Broom: Cut stems under water and condition in hot water. Can have an unpleasant odor. Dries successfully. All parts cause severe discomfort if ingested.

GENTIANA andrewsii Bottle gentian: Cut stems under water and condition in cool water. Long lasting.

Geranium: see PELARGONIUM.

GERBERA African daisy: Cut stems under water, boil or burn stems 15 seconds and condition in cool water. Support flower heads in conditioning bucket to prevent stems from bending.

Ginger, european: see ASARUM europaeum.

Ginger, tropical: see ALPINUS purpurata.

Ginger, torch: see ETLINGERA elatior.

GLADIOLUS: Cut stems under water and condition in warm vinegar water. Remove the tight buds at the top (they probably will not open) to encourage opening of flowers. Long lasting.

GLORIOSA lily: Cut stems under water and condition in cool water. All parts toxic.

GODETIA grandiflora: Cut stems under water and condition in warm water. Long lasting.

Goldenrod: see SOLIDAGO.

GOMPHRENA Globe amaranth: Pick in full color. Boil stems and condition in cool vinegar water. Air dry, preserves well and holds color.

Grasses: Remove bottom white part of stems. Submerge in cool water one hour, remove and condition in warm vinegar water. Tend to dry out quickly.

GYPSOPHILA paniculata Baby's breath: Cut stems under water and condition in hot water; avoid wetting blossoms. Hydrate in a separate bucket, tends to foul conditioning water. Long lasting. Tends to have an unpleasant odor when used in large quantities. Air dry.

HAMAMELIS cv. Witch hazel: Crush or cross-cut stems, peel bark 1"-2" and condition in hot water. Long lasting. Forces successfully.

Heather: see CALLUNA.

HEDERA helix Ivy: Submerge in cool water for two hours, remove and place in a sealed plastic bag. Keep in a cool, dark area. Long lasting. All parts toxic. Sap may irritate skin. All parts cause severe discomfort if ingested.

HELIANTHUS cv. Sunflower: Cut stems under water, boil stem ends and condition in warm vinegar water. If flowers are large, support with wire through stem. Does not last long.

HELIANTHUS tuberosus Jerusalem artichoke: Cut stems under water, boil cuts and condition in warm vinegar water.

HELICONIA caribea Wild plantain: Do not refrigerate, keep in warm (55-60 degrees F.) and very humid area. Avoid drafts and heat sources. Cut stems under water and condition in room temperature water to keep stem ends from drying out. Spray with fixative before arranging. Floral preservatives are unnecessary because stems take up very little water. Long lasting, 2-3 weeks.
Note: flowers remain at the stage in which they are cut, they do not continue to develop.

HELICONIA rostrata Hanging heliconia: see H. caribea. Lasts less than 14 days.

HELICONIA humilis Lobster claw heliconia: see H. caribea. Very long lasting, 4 weeks.

HELLEBORUS: Cut stems under water and hold ends in boiling water. Prick stems in many spots, condition in deep water. All parts are toxic.

HEMEROCALLIS Daylily: Cut stems under water and condition in cool vinegar water. A new flower opens daily and lasts only one day.

93

Herbs: Submerge entire stem one hour. Remove, cut stems under water and condition in cool water. Keep in a damp cloth in a cool, dark area. Test before using.

HEUCHERA Coral bells: Cut stems under water and condition in cool water. Long lasting.

HIPPEASTRUM Amaryllis: Cut stems under water and condition in cool vinegar water. When arranging, insert stake up stem to flower head for support. Long lasting in floral foam.

Holly: see ILEX.

Honesty: see LUNERIA.

HOSTA Plantain lily, funkia: Submerge leaves in cool water for two hours. Remove and condition in cool water. Use only mature growth, new spring leaves will wilt. Long lasting.

HYACINTHUS garden hyacinth: Remove white portion of stem, it does not take up water. Cut stems under water and condition in cool water. Do not condition with other flowers, it tends to foul the water.

HYDRANGEA: Remove all foliage, submerge flower 1/2 hour in cool water. Remove, crush or cross-cut stems, peel bark 1"-2" and condition in hot vinegar water. To preserve, pick when flower is desired color, keep in a warm area with stems in a small amount of water until dry; or, hang, out of water, to dry.

HYPERICUM St. Johns wort: Cut stems under water and condition in warm water. Long lasting.

IBERIS sempervirens Candytuft, perennial: Cut stems under water and condition in cool water.

ILEX Holly: Submerge entire branch in cool water one hour. Remove, crush or cross-cut stems, peel bark 1"-2" and condition in hot water. Do not place near fruit or orchids. Does not last long.

ILEX verticillata Winterberry: Remove leaves in the fall; use red berries on branches out of water. Long lasting

IRIS: Pick in bud, remove white bottom portion of stem as water only travels up the green part. Cut stems under water and condition in cool water. Remove each flower as it fades to encourage buds to open. Can be held two-three days by picking in bud with small amount of color showing, wrap in wet newspaper and keep in a cool and dark area. When time to arrange, condition as above. Does not last long.

Ivy: see HEDERA helix.

IXIA Corn lily: Cut stems under water and condition in cool water. Long lasting.

Jerusalem artichoke: see HELIANTHUS tuberosus.

Joe Pye weed: see EUPATORIUM purpureum.

Jonquil: see NARCISSUS.

KALANCOE: This succulent is best used as a plant. It is very tolerant of light and humidity, lasting a long time in full bloom.

KALMIA latifolia cv. Mountain laurel: Crush or cross-cut stems, peel bark 1"-2" and condition in hot water. Does not last long.

Kangaroo-paw: see ANIGOZANTHOS cv.

KERRIA japonica cv. Kerria: Submerge entire branch 1/2 hour in cool water, cut stems under water and condition in hot water. Long lasting.

KNIPHOFIA Red-hot poker: Cut stems under water and condition in room temperature water.

Lady's mantle: see ALCHEMILLA mollis.

Lamb's ears: see STACHYS byzantina cv.

LAMIUM maculatum Spotted deadnettle: Submerge entire stem for one hour, remove and condition in cool water. Long lasting.

Larkspur: see CONSOLIDA.

LATHYRUS odoratus Sweet pea: Cut stems under water and condition in cool, grain alcohol water. Avoid water on petals. Can be used out of water for several hours after conditioning. Generally does not last long. If seeds are ingested they may cause discomfort.

Lemon leaf: see CITRUS limon.

LEPTOSPERMUM Tea tree: Crush or cross-cut stems and condition in hot water.

Leucadendron: see PROTEA.

Leucospermum: see PROTEA.

Lettuce, leaf: Submerge in cool water for one hour, remove and wrap in moist, porous cloth; keep in refrigerator. Lasts several hours when used in an arrangement.

LEUCOTHOE: Condition in warm water, extremly long lasting.

LIATRIS cv.: Cut stems under water and condition in warm water. Long lasting.

Lilac: see SYRINGA.

LILIUM cv. Lily: Cut stems under water and condition in cool water. Remove pollen as each flower opens (pollen matures flower and stains clothing - carefully remove pollen on clothing with sticky tape, do not rub). Long lasting.
To encourage buds to open, pass buds under tepid water; place stems in warm water and gently break seals between petals.

Lily: see LILIUM cv.

Lily grass: see OPHIOPOGON sp.

Lily-of-the-valley: see CONVALLARIA cv.

LIMONIUM latifolium Sea lavender: Cut stems under water and condition in warm water. Long lasting.

LIMONIUM sinuatum Statice: Cut stems under water and condition in warm water. Very long lasting. Air dry.

Lisianthus: see EUSTOMA grandiflorum cv.

Loosestrife, purple: see LYTHRUM salicaria 'Atropurpureum'

LUNARIA Honesty, money plant: Cut stems under water and condition flower stems in hot water. Or, use dry when seed pods appear; remove outer casing by gently rubbing between forefinger and thumb to reveal shiny silver dollars.

LUPINUS cv. Lupine: Pick when only three rings of flowers are open, use hollow-stem treatment and condition in cool water. Can be dried in silica gel. Discomfort caused if seeds are ingested.

LYCOPODIUM: Do not refrigerate, this is tropical foliage. Cut stems under water, wrap in damp newspaper and condition in room temperature water so that newspaper acts like a wick to keep foliage from drying out; cover bucket with plastic. Lasts 7-10 days from picking time.

LYSIMACHIA Loosestrife: Cut stems under water and condition in warm water.

LYTHRUM salicaria 'Atropurpureum' Loosestrife, purple: Cut stems under water and condition in warm water.

MAGNOLIA grandiflora Southern magnolia: Crush or cross-cut stems, peel bark 1"-2" and condition in hot water.

MAHONIA aquifolium Oregon grapeholly: Crush or cross-cut stems and condition in hot water. Can be preserved in glycerin.

MALUS Apple, crabapple: Cut in bud and submerge entire branch in cool water for one hour. Remove and crush or cross-cut stems, peel bark 1" - 2" and condition in hot water. Forces well.

Maple, Japanese: see ACER palmatum.

Marguerite: see CHRYSANTHEMUM leucanthemum

Marigold: see TAGETES.

MATTHIOLA incana Stock: Crush or cross-cut stems, boil or burn cuts and condition in cold water in a separate bucket. Does not last long.

MENTHA Mint: Submerge in cool water one hour, condition in cool water or wrap in porous, damp cloth and place in refrigerator. Can be air dried.

Michaelmas Daisy, Aster: see ASTER cv.

Mimosa: see ACACIA.

Ming Fern: see ASPARAGUS densiflorus cv.

Mint: see MENTHA.

Mock orange: see PHILADELPHUS.

MOLUCCELLA laevis Bells of Ireland: Remove leaves. Cut stems under water and condition in cool water. Long lasting. Air dry.

Money plant: see LUNARIA.

Monkshood: see ACONITUM.

97

Montbretia: see TRITONIA.

Monte Cassino: see ASTER pringlei 'Monte Cassino'

Mountain Laurel: see KALMIA latifolia cv.

MUSA cv. Banana plant: Cut stems under water and condition in warm water. Apply vinegar to cut edges to discourage discoloring. Spray with fixative.

NARCISSUS Daffodil: Remove white portion of stem as water only travels up the green part. Cut stems under water and condition in cool alcohol water in a separate bucket (tends to foul conditioning water). Does not last long. Foliage, sap and bulb may irritate skin.

Nasturtium: see TROPAEOLUM.

NERINE: Cut stems under water and condition in cool water. Very long lasting.

NYMPHAEA Water lily: Fill hollow stems with pond water or grain alcohol and plug with cotton. Wire stems. Carefully drop warm paraffin or glue between petals to keep them open. Conditioning is very difficult and you are fortunate if your flower lasts one day. Keep stems short, the closer the lily is to water the happier it will be.

Oak: see QUERCUS.

Obedient plant: see PHYSOSTEGIA.

ONCIMUM basilicum Sweet basil: Cut stems under water, submerge in cool water. Best used in cooking. Air dry or freeze.

Onion/chives: see ALLIUM.

OPHIOPOGON sp. Lily grass: Submerge under water one hour, remove bottom white part of stem, cut stems under water and condition in warm water.

ORCHIDS: Often orchids come in water vials; keep in vials and replenish water with floral preservative in vials as necessary. Mist flowers, place in plastic bag and keep at 45-55 degrees F. AVOID STORING NEAR FRESH FRUITS AND VEGETABLES, avoid drafts and heat sources.

Remove old flowers as they die.

       Cattleya - Lasts 4-5 days; mist with water and keep cool.
       Phalaenopsis/moth orchid - Lasts 4-5 days; mist with water and keep cool.
       Vanda - Some varieties may last 3 weeks. Very sensitive to ethylene gas.
       Cymbidium - Lasts 7-10 days.
       Dendrobium - Different varieties last from 7-10 days. Not sensitive to ethylene gas.
       Oncidium - Lasts 7-10 days, some varieties may last 3 weeks. Not sensitive to ethylene gas.

ORNITHOGALUM sp. Star-of-Bethlehem: Cut stems under water and condition in cool water. Long lasting.

PACHYSANDRA: Submerge in cool water for two hours. Remove and seal in a plastic bag. Store in refrigerator. Long lasting.

PAEONIA japonica Common garden peony: Cut in bud with color showing, remove foliage, rinse sticky substance from bud (this is usually done by ants on peonies from an outdoor garden). Cut stems under water and condition in warm, sugar water.
Can be held successfully up to two weeks - cut in bud with color showing, do not remove leaves, cover with damp newspaper and place in cool, damp area (cellar floor). When it is time to arrange peonies, first proceed with the above conditioning.

Pansy: see VIOLA cv.

PAPAVER Poppy: Pick when bud is showing color. Boil cut and condition in cool water. Does not last long.

Papyrus: see CYPERUS papyrus.

Parsley: see PETROCELINUM.

Peace lily: see SPATHIPHYLLUM cv.

Peach: see PRUNUS.

PELARGONIUM Geranium: Cut stems under water. Boil or burn stem ends and condition in warm water. Spray with fixative after arranging.

Peony: see PAEONIA.

PETROCELINUM Parsley: Submerge under cool water for one hour, remove and keep in a porous, damp cloth in the refrgerator; or store in a glass of cool water. Long lasting.

PHILADELPHUS Mock orange: Crush or cross-cut stems, peel bark 1"-2" and condition in hot water. Flowers do not last long.

PHILODENDRON: Cut stems under water and condition in warm water. Long lasting. Sap may irritate skin. Discomfort caused if any part is ingested.

PHLOX: see PHLOX paniculata.

PHLOX paniculata Garden phlox: Cut stems under water and condition in cool water. Does not last long.

PHYSOSTEGIA Obedient plant: Cut stems under water and condition in cool water. Long lasting.

PHYTOLACCA americana Pokeweed: Cut stems under water and condition in warm water. Poisonous berries, do not use near food. All parts toxic. Sap may irritate skin.

PIERIS floribunda Mountain pieris, andromeda: Crush or cross-cut stems, peel bark 1"-2" and condition in hot water. Long lasting. Evergreen; flowers force successfully.

PIERIS japonica Lily-of-the-valley bush: Crush or cross-cut stems, peel bark 1"-2" and condition in hot water. Long lasting. Evergreen; flowers force successfully.

Pineapple: see ANANAS bracteatus.

Pitcher-Plant: see Sarracenia drummondi.

PITTOSPORUM: Condition in hot water, mist. Long lasting.

Plantain lily: see HOSTA.

Plum. flowering: see PRUNUS.

PODOCARPUS: Do not refrigerate, this is tropical foliage. Crush or cross-cut stems, condition in warm water and cover bucket with plastic. Very long lasting, 3 weeks or more.

Poinsettia: see EUPHORBIA pulcherrima.

Pokeweed: see PHYTOLACCA americana.

POLIANTHES tuberosa cv. Tuberose: Boil cut stem and condition in cool water. Prick stem with pin just below flower head to release air. Remove brown outside petals as they appear. Very fragrant. Long lasting.

POLYGONATUM biflorum Solomon's seal: Cut stems under water and condition in cool water. Long lasting.

POLYSCIAS quilfoylei Coffee tree: Crush or cross-cut stems and condition in hot water. Does not last long.

Poppy: see Papaver.

Poppy anemone, wind flower: see ANEMONE.

PROTEA: Remove only the foliage that will be under water. Cut stems under water and condition in warm water (100-110 degrees F.) with preservative added. Keep in a humid, 45-50 degrees F. area away from heat and drafts. Add water with preservative frequently and recut stems when possible. Do not treat these flowers like succulents!

There are many proteas with flower heads ranging from 3 inches in diameter to the King protea that can have a flower head with a diameter of 12 inches. This genus is long lasting, 10-20 days.

Leucadendron is a large variety ranging in use from the flowers to "filler" foliage. Long lasting, 28-42 days.

Leucospermum or the Sunburst Proteas such as the Pincushion last 7-14 days.
Banksia spikes, long lasting 10-20 days.

Preserve proteas by drying. Remove flowers from water a few days before their prime and hang or allow to stand upright in a container. To preserve in glycerin solution, see section on Preserving Flowers and Leaves.

PRUNUS Almond, cherry, peach, plum: Submerge entire branch in room temperature water one hour. Remove, crush or cross-cut stems, peel bark 1"-2" and condition in hot water. Ornamental flowering plums force successfully. Blossoms do not last long.

Pussy Willow: see Salix discolor.

Queen Ann's-Lace: see ANTHRISCUS sylvestris.

QUERCUS Oak: Crush or cross-cut stems, peel bark 1"-2" and condition in hot water. Can be preserved in glycerine; use small leaves and pick before leaves turn red in the fall.

Quince, Japanese flowering: see CHAENOMELES japonica.

RANUNCULUS Buttercup: Boil cut stems and condition in cool water. Does not last long.

Red-hot poker: see KNIPHOFIA.

Redbud: see CERCIS canadensis.

Redtwig dogwood: see CORNUS.

RHODODENDRON: Crush or cross-cut stems, peel bark 1"-2" and condition in hot sugar and vinegar water.

RHODODENDRON japonicum Japanese Azalea: Pick in bud, crush or cross-cut stems, peel bark 1"-2" and condition in hot sugar and vinegar water. Does not last long. Forces well.

RHUS Sumac: When leaves turn red in the fall condition in hot salt water. Does not last long. Best to use red seed pods as dry material. WARNING: some Sumac is poisonous.

ROSA Rose: Cut off leaves, strip only the thorns that will interfere with arranging (any cut in the stem makes an open wound for moisture to escape). Remove outside dry petals on buds; CUT STEMS UNDER WATER and condition in warm water with preservative added.
Arrange in water (floral foam may not provide enough water for thirsty roses).
After conditioning, roses can last six hours out of water. Dry in silica gel.

Rose hips the "fruit" of the rose: Cut in autumn when hips are red and leaves have fallen. Use out of water; will stay fresh outside all winter.

RUDBECKIA coneflower Brown-eyed Susan: Submerge flower head in cool water for one hour. Remove, cut stems under water and condition in warm water. Preserve in silica gel.

RUMEX Dock: Pick in green, pink or brown stage. Condition in warm water. Long lasting. Air dry.

RUSCUS, Italian and Swedish: Cut stems under water and condition in warm water. Long lasting.

Safflower: see CARTHEMUS tinctorius.

Sago Palm: see CYCUS.

SALIX discolor Pussy willow: Condition in hot water. Leaves tend to be buggy. Remove leaves to use dry.

SALIX matsudana 'Tortuosa' Corkscrew willow: Crush or cross-cut stem, boil cut and condition in hot water. Forces successfully, leaves tend to be buggy.
Corkscrew and fasciated willow are best used as a bare branches in line designs.

SALVIA sage: Cut stems under water and condition in warm alcohol water. Blue annual air drys successfully.

SARRACENIA Pitcher-plant: Fill hollow flower with room temperature water and condition in cool water. Keep in a warm and humid area. This plant grows in warm, swampy locations. Does not last long. Can be dried.

SCIADOPITYS verticillata Japanese umbrella pine: Crush or cross-cut stems and condition in hot water. Very long lasting.

Sea lavender: see LIMONIUM latifolium.

SEDUM: Cut under water and condition in cool water. Long lasting.

September Weed: see ASTER.

SKIMMIA: Crush or cross-cut stems and condition in hot water.

SMILAX: Submerge in room temperature water for two hours. Remove, seal in a plastic sack and keep in the refrigerator. Will last out of water in an arrangement for 10 -12 hours

Smokebush, Purple: see COTINUS coggygria 'Royal Purple'.

Snapdragon: see ANTIRRHINUM.

Snowball Tree: see VIBURNUM cv.

SOLIDAGO Goldenrod: Pick when two-thirds in bloom. Cut stems under water and condition in warm water. Long lasting. Air dry. Non-allergic.

Solomon's seal: see POLYGONATUM biflorum.

SPATHIPHYLLUM Peace lily: Cut stems under water and condition in warm water. Long lasting.

Spider Flower: see CLEOME.

SPIRAEA prunifolia Spirea, Bridalwreath: Cut in bud. Submerge entire branch in cool water, remove and condition in hot water. Does not last long.

103

Sprengeri: see ASPARAGUS densiflorus.

STACHYS olympica Lambs' ears: Cut stems under water and condition in warm water. Do not allow water to get on furry leaves. Long lasting.

Star-of-Bethlehem: see ORNITHOGALUM.

Statice: see LIMONIUM sinuatum.

St. John's wort: see HYPERICUM.

Stock: see MATTHIOLA incana.

STRELITZIA reginae Bird of paradise: Do not refrigerate, keep in warm (45-50 degrees F.) and humid area. Cut stems under water and condition in warm water with preservative added. Avoid drafts and extremes in temperature. Long lasting, 7-14 days.
A fresh stem from a plant grown in optimum conditions will contain 4-5 'birds'."Cut Bird-of-paradise flowers do not usually emerge from the sheath on their own. To open, soak flower head in room temperature water for about 20 minutes. Make a 1/2" slit at back end of pod near stem. Reach in with your thumb and carefully lift out the petals. Hold the pod at the bottom and gently pull up the new blossoms into a fan."[1]

SUCCULENTS Stapelia, Aloe and Haworthia genera: Most store water in their plant tissue which makes them useful for designs out of water. Long lasting.

Sumac: see RHUS.

Sunflower: see HELIANTHUS cv.

Sweet Pea: see LATHYRUS odoratus.

SYRINGA Lilac: Remove all leaves except the tiny top leaves against the flower head, carefully submerge flower head (or entire stem if possible) in cool water for two hours. Remove, crush or cross-cut stem and condition in hot water overnight. Spray flower head with fixative. Does not force well; flowers will be smaller than normal and dull in color.

TAGETES Marigold: Cut stems under water and condition in cool water in a separate bucket (tends to foul conditioning water). Dry for potpourri, excellent color, scent disappears..

TANACETUM parthenium Feverfew: Cut stems under water and condition in cool water. Long lasting.

TANACETUM vulgare Tansy: Pick in full bloom, cut stems under water and condition in warm water. Long lasting. Air dries successfully.

Tansy: see TANACETUM vulgare.

Thistle: see ECHINOPS.

Ti: see CORDYLINE terminalis.

TRITONIA Montbretia, crocosmia: Cut stems under water and condition in cool water. Long lasting.

TROPAEOLUM Nasturtium: Cut stems under water and condition in cool water. A beautiful addition to the garden salad.

Tuberose: see POLIANTHES tuberosa cv.

TULIPA Tulip: Remove white portion of stem end as water travels up only the green part. Cut stems under water and condition in cool water. Addition of grain alcohol to the conditioning water makes the stems rigid.
Before arranging, prick stem with a pin just below the flower head; doing this slows maturing and decreases tendency for growth; a tulip stem can grow one inch per day after it is picked. Dutch tulips do not last long. French tulips are long lasting. Foliage may irritate skin. All parts cause severe discomfort if ingested.

TYPHA Cattail: Cut when color is beginning to change from green to brown, early summer. Spray with fixative or acrylic. Do not save if brown tails begin to split; cotton-like seeds from one cattail will fill a room 9' x 12' x 8'!

Umbrella Pine: see SCIADOPITYS verticillata.

VACCINIUM corymbosum Highbush blueberry: Crush or cross-cut stems, peel bark 1" - 2" and condition in hot salt water. Fall red foliage holds better in salt water, but still does not last long.

Vegetable greens: Submerge one hour in cool water. Remove and wrap in damp, porous cloth. Keep in refrigerator. Not long lasting.

VERONICA: Cut stems under water and condition in cool water.

VIBURNUM cv. Chinese snowball: Submerge flower heads for one hour. Remove, cut stems under water and condition in hot water. Does not last long.

VIOLA cv. Violet: Submerge in cool water fifteen minutes. Remove, cut stems under water and condition in cool water. Arrange in clusters. Does not last long.

VIOLA cv. Pansy: Cut stems under water and arrange in cool water. Does not last long.

Violet: see VIOLA cv.

Water Lily: see NYMPHAEA cv.

WATSONIA: Cut stems under water and condition in cool water.

Willow, corkscrew: see SALIX matsudana 'Tortuosa'.

Winterberry: see ILEX verticillata.

WISTERIA: Submerge flower one hour in cool water. Remove from bath; crush or cross-cut stem and boil cut. Stand in pure grain alcohol for 1/2 hour, condition in hot water. Does not last long. All parts cause severe discomfort if ingested

Witch Hazel: see HAMAMELIS cv.

Yarrow: see ACHILLEA.

ZANTEDESCHIA Calla Lily : Cut stems under water and condition in cool water. Long lasting. Sap may irritate skin. All parts cause severe discomfort if ingested.

ZINNIA: Cut stems under water and condition in cool water in a separate bucket; tends to foul conditioning water. Does not last long.

[1]Adelheid R. Kuehnle, PhD *Tropical Flowers and Tropical Foliage*

Acknowledgments

I am very happy to have been able to volunteer at the Museum of Fine Arts, Boston, where I have had the opportunity to practice flower design both for the enjoyment of the public and for the critical eyes of my peers. In writing this book, I have drawn heavily upon the experience of the Ladies Committee, and I wish to thank my fellow members for their help in sharing this wealth of knowledge with you — particularly Nancy Bates, Mary Cannon, Marilyn MacLellan, and Dede Woods. A special thanks to Nancy McMahon and Kathy Thomas for editing and proof reading the text. I am also very grateful to the scores of Garden Club arrangers who have made Art in Bloom at the Museum possible and, in doing so, have increased our understanding and enjoyment of floral design.

Bibliography

Arms, **John Taylor and Dorothhy Noyes**. *DESIGN IN FLOWER ARRANGE-MENT.* New York, The MACMILLAN COMPANY, 1937

Ascher, Amalie Adler. *The Complete Flower Arranger.*

Belcher, Betty. *Creative Flower Arranging.* Timber Press, Portland, Oregon, 1993

Berrall, Julia S. *The Garden*, New York, A Studio Book, The Viking Press, 1966

Clayton, John. *Flower Arranging.* GALLERY BOOKS, W.H. SMITH, NEW YORK, 1985

Floralife, inc. Burr Ridge, Illinois, 1997

Garden Club of America. *Flower Show and Judging Guide,* 1997

Girard, Sarah. COLOR THEORY, Studio Course, Harvard School of Design

National Council of State Garden Clubs, Inc. *Handbook for Flower Shows,* 1997

Horticulture, The Art of American Gardening, 1984-1997

Hynson, Sandra S. *Flowers to the Glory of God.* Felfoot Publishers, Keedysville, Maryland 1990

Kuehnle, Adelheid R. PhD. Department of Horticulture, University of Hawaii at Manoa, 1997

Macqueen, Sheila. *Complete Flower Arranging.*

Massachusetts Horticultural Society, Nomeclature, 1997

Massachusetts Horticultural Society, Plant Label Guidelines, 1997

Mid-Kent College, U.K. *Chelsea Flower Show 1999*

North Shore Garden Club. *Tips on preparing cut flowers;* pamphlet

The American Horticultural Society. *A-Z Encyclopedia of Garden Plants* 1997

Pokon & Chrysal. *For Complete Plant and Flower Care.* Naarden, Holland, 1997

Smithers-Oasis U.S.A. 1997

Taylor, Norman, *Encyclopedia of Gardening.* Houghton Mifflin Company, Boston 1961